The Empire Has No Clothes
Observations on life, humanity, and America
by someone who missed the announcement

by Grieg Pedersen

ISBN
Paperback: 978-0-9991301-0-0
Kindle: 978-0-9991301-1-7

First Edition: July 2017

Dedication

To my wife, Nancy, for her godlike patience.

To my many friends and as many random turns of fate,
without whom many of these things would have gone unnoticed.

And to my daughter Aurora,
without whose insightful questions and artistic talent
this book would have neither voice nor form.

Observations

Before I Begin

"It is the mark of an educated mind to be able to consider an idea without having to accept it."

- *Aristotle*

Let's agree to do that, okay? It'll make things go a lot more smoothly. I see things differently in part because I've seen a lot, in part because I have Asperger's Syndrome (AS), and in part because I'm just odd. I hate the word "syndrome" because it sounds ominous, threatening. Some call it "Geek Syndrome," but I prefer "Nerds' Disease." Disease seems less harsh to me than Syndrome, and that's the opposite of some other people, probably because I've had so little disease in my life. Lucky. Some people passionately hate the word disease, probably because they've seen enough of it already. I just find I can't take "syndrome" lightly enough.   A disease seems curable, but a syndrome seems intractable. All that said, my AS isn't a syndrome or a disease to me. It's a blessing. I can make models of things in my head, set them running, and look for problems. I've designed and tested things in a few minutes that took hours or days to get on paper afterward so I can show them to others. It's also a curse. It comes with a set of inabilities that most people would find bewildering. I have had to learn to read body language *consciously*.   I can't describe people in physical terms – I took to memorizing certain specific characteristics of my wife's appearance (height and other dimensions, hair color, eye color) by rote because after

1

THE EMPIRE HAS NO CLOTHES!

17 years of marriage I still couldn't just do it. I often don't recognize people I don't know well. I have no idea where I stand with you most of the time, but strangely it seems I can tell where you stand with each other fairly well.

Much of that curse I've been able to use to my advantage, because I can see now how many people see things, even if I can't see them that way myself. If I had to give up the advantages to be rid of the difficulties, I wouldn't do it. My other insights are more important to me than knowing if she's "into me."

There's a thing I call The High Llama Syndrome that explains the path to many of my views, and also why some people can agree at the top of their lungs – or not know that they dangerously disagree. A character from an old comic strip, the "high llama" sits high atop his mountain thinking about life. Each thought builds on the previous one, and changes it. In the end, a simple sentence (not from the comic strip) explains everything:

"Life is a little blue bird chirping in a cinnamon tree." - The High Llama

Yeah, right. That may mean a lot to the High Llama, but it means nothing to me. The llama (maybe I'm the one who's high?) tells me that when I achieve enlightenment I'll understand. You see, it's important that the bird is little and it's blue, and that it's a cinnamon tree, and that the bird is chirping rather than singing. All of that is vitally important – not to understanding life, but to understanding all the extra layers of meaning that the High Llama has piled on to each of those words in that context.

We all do it. If I say the word delicious, what does your mind conjure up? A taste, almost certainly, perhaps many; perhaps a smell; perhaps even the image of the delicious thing you're tasting in your memory. Perhaps even the sights, sounds, smells, and all the context of last time you experienced it. A food, a drink, a lover, an irony, each of us experiences the word delicious very differently from everyone else, and even differently in different situations. We rely on the dictionary for the literal meaning of words and on the Empire for other meanings, and we

2

tell stories to explain our personal meanings. When we forget about the stories and judge others' words or reactions on our own personal layers of meaning, we suffer the High Llama Syndrome.

It'll happen here, I'm sure. An entire episode of *Star Trek: The Next Generation* revolved around this, and the metaphor for it was metaphor itself. I leave you with "Darmok and Jalad at Tanagra."

All of you will likely disagree with me somewhere. In fact, I'm pretty sure just about all of you will get mad at me at some point. After all, I don't think there's even one thing that everyone can agree on (more on that later). I'm also pretty sure that each of you will agree with me here and there. There's a lot here, and it's a whole package. It really does work together well for me. I hope you'll consider all of it, even if I'm not right everywhere or you see things differently. This is, after all, just my perspective. This is how I see the Empire, and The Empire's New Clothes, and why I get nervous when those clothes change.

Missing the Announcement

No one ever told me that the Empire had clothes. For many, many years it never occurred to me to point that out to anyone because I never thought of it. That the Empire has no clothes was neither a revelation nor a surprise to me. What came as a surprise was finding out that the vast majority of the Empire's subjects thought it did. From there it took me a long time to work out what those clothes were and how to tell people.

We all see the same things, but we interpret them differently. Many "enlightened" people today deride our ancient forbears for their belief in four elements: earth, water, air, and fire. After all, look at the periodic table and those four are nowhere to be seen. "Our ancestors were idiots!" we cry. Except that they weren't. They saw something profound, and simply misinterpreted it. They thought that what they were looking at were the four things everything is made of. In fact what they were observing were the four states all things exist in: solid, liquid, gas, and plasma. This is one way the Empire's clothes get made.

When the Empire's clothes suddenly change we need to be very cautious. It happens a lot when nations go to war, when regimes change, or when someone wants to channel an old cultural habit to a new purpose. Any time that happens, look at both sets of clothes, new and old, and ask yourself what they're really covering and whose tailor is behind the change. The Empire's clothes are changing a lot lately, and I don't expect that to stop or even slow down as long as people still see the

Empire's new clothes.

When you cry out that the Emperor is naked, do try to be sure you're not just seeing another set of clothes. My best illustration of that is the aliens at Roswell. That thing with the weather balloon or UFO all happened near the first Air Force base to have nuclear weapons. I think someone had a clever idea that you can't use too often: two cover stories. The Manhattan Project was a big, expensive, secret project to create the atomic bomb. I don't think that that was the only thing that got funded. A radical new weapon might just warrant a radical new delivery system. So what if what crashed was part of that: an attempt at a nuclear drone of some sort? It crashes and they say, "UFO!" Then they say, "weather balloon!" For the next 60 years, everyone debates whether it's a UFO or a weather balloon, when in fact it may have been a failed and very expensive black project. That "memory metal" sounds a lot like aluminized mylar to me, and it was officially invented just a few years later.

What is the Empire?

It's a lot of things, but it isn't some global conspiracy to keep you down. It doesn't have to be, because it works perfectly well at that without being one. It's a whole lot of self-interest by a whole lot of people who aren't you. It's there because it's worked for a long time, but the upheaval we're now seeing in all aspects of life tell me that the Empire is changing, a lot of little Emperors are falling from power, and they're changing clothes to try to hold on. The Empire is your culture, government, language, society, economy... anything and everything that makes demands on the way you live and tries to conform you into a particular way of acting, and more importantly, thinking.

Value of Empire

The Empire has value. It makes laws and rules to keep people from harming each other, and makes it possible to punish those who do without society falling into an eternal cycle of revenge. It sets guidelines and helps people know what's rude or offensive, so they can avoid them and carry on civil conversations, exchange ideas, and benefit from them. As Joseph Campbell observed, myth is the carrier of morality in most cultures. That's fine, but I think it's time we start moving beyond that. We can still have our Michael Crichtons telling us cautionary tales[1], but in the end we really ought to base what we believe on what we know, not try to make it the other way around.

Price of Empire

All magic comes at a price, and the Empire is no exception. The Empire tells you that to matter, you must own a house, a nice car (not just any car), get married, and have 2.1 kids. You must get a college education so you can work for a good company and it will take care of you. You must specialize, you have to pick your career in high school, you have to have one overriding passion, success is only measured in money, cut your grass this way, have grass at all, wear the right clothes, wear clothes at all, be single, get married, you can love only one person (got kids?)...

The Empire's New Clothes

The Empire is made up of all the things that help and pressure you to fit in, to be productive, to follow the rules, and quash your individuality. The Empire's clothes are the made-up reasons you've been told to believe about why that's supposed to be good for you. Some of those reasons are legit, but mostly they're just myths to back up the fact that we've "always" done it this way, even though we haven't. Sometimes a myth might be good for you, and for us, and sometimes it isn't. You can decide which is which for you, but The Empire's New Clothes need to be shown for what they are: stories we tell ourselves to confirm our own sense of rightness.

My outlook has always been quite different. In kindergarten I was

---

1   The Andromeda Strain, Westworld, Jurassic Park, and so many others. Fortunately for us he was never the only one.

ridiculed for being more interested in how the wheels worked than in the fact that the toy was a fire truck. Later I was ridiculed for my intelligence (and probably my misfitness). That was fine. It didn't matter. Their petty concern with obviously temporary social status didn't matter, just like their obsession with "stuff" didn't matter. They still don't. I've had the good fortune to use my so-called disorder to build a remarkable career and focus not on the individual things but on how they fit together. My dad noticed that and complimented me on it – once. To him, having said it meant that it was true until he said otherwise. It wasn't ever necessary to repeat it. I quickly noticed that that isn't how most people work. Most people, whom we aspies call "neurotypical," need to have that kind of thing reinforced verbally on a regular basis. So do I, but I suppose my idea of a regular basis can survive a longer drought than most. I'm comfortable with who I am and I don't define myself in terms of my culture or its expectations. I've given up on the Empire and the Imperial System. I guess you could say I've gone Metric. Really I was born Metric, and it took me a while to notice the presence of the Empire.

How did the Empire's clothes come to be? Well, there are a lot of ways. Sometimes it's just what we assume other people think. Sometimes it's the Victorians creating bogus images of the Plymouth pilgrims to make them seem more familiar. Sometimes it's a glossing over of the bad parts of history or amplifying someone else's bad parts to create a comfortable superiority. Sometimes, like the Earth, Water, Air, and Fire, we just get our interpretations wrong. The clothes build up over time, and as culture gradually changes, the clothes naturally change, too. We all participate in the making of the Empire's new clothes, whether we mean to or not, and social media is making that happen so much faster than it used to. It used to be primarily a generational thing; now it can happen in days. Beware the sudden changing of the Empire's clothes!

If we need to be wary of rapidly changing clothes, we need to know how to spot them in the first place! That's not easy. Your first hint is "that's just the way it is." If you hear that, or "it's always been that way," or "it's a fundamental property of the universe," or even, "isn't it obvious," it means they don't know why; and when they're trying to tell you why things are and they don't know the why behind it, that's a pretty good hint. At least if they admit they don't know why, and maybe offer a few possibilities, then at least you know they're actually thinking about it.

When you're looking at what might be the Empire's New Clothes, there are a lot of things to look out for: rhetorical tools, emotional appeals, and logical fallacies of all kinds. All of these things appeal to our own internal biases, and we have a lot of them. The two biggest are Confirmation Bias and Saliency Bias. Confirmation bias is when we give more weight to new information or ideas that agree with what we already think, and dismiss those that disagree. Saliency bias is another tricky one: we're a lot more likely to accept an idea if we understand it and dismiss it if we don't. It's not that the idea isn't right; we just don't get it, and rather than go to the effort of working through it we tend to just ignore it. It's hard not to do these, but being aware of them helps. Beware: people on every side of life will use these against you!

The "rule of three" is a big emotional tool people use to convince you. They use exactly three examples, reasons, or whatever.[2] Even if they have to repeat one of them, say something irrelevant, or make one up.[3]

Another thing the Empire likes to do is pick out a couple of examples and say things like "see? PROOF!" and "if they can do it, anyone can," and "conspiracy." The problem with that is, often the examples chosen are what statisticians call outliers. When I was a kid we called them "the exception that proves the rule." People like to pick a few of these exceptions and think – or pretend – that they're the rule.

The Empire's clothes are often made up of stories we tell ourselves because we don't know the truth. They fill in for things we don't know, but then when we do find out we cling to the old myths rather than accept the truth. Sometimes we invent myths to protect ourselves from

---

2   See what I did there?
3   Did it again! Care to go for three?

the truths we don't want to face. Let evidence be your guide, and check your sources.

The Empire's clothes are also made up of stories we're told by someone who wants us to forget about the truth, or not see it, or promote their own self-worth. Alternative facts are not facts at all. I'm entitled to my own opinions, but not to my own facts. At all times, know that the Empire's clothes are there to hide the facts, known or unknown. Sometimes that's nefarious, sometimes innocent, and sometimes it's just made of what we assume others think.

There's a wonderful web site called YourLogicalFallacyIs.com. They have a poster and a useful key to spotting logical fallacies like straw men (creating a fatally flawed copy of what you're arguing against and then using that flaw to "push the straw man over"), ad hominem (attacking the source instead of the argument), and everyone's favorite: picking out the outliers in the data and misrepresenting them as the trend. They call it "Texas Sharpshooter." It's a good guide, and it's not the only one out there.

Lemming Illuminati

Social pressure has a way of keeping people in line, of keeping the extreme among us from getting too far out, but it also keeps us from thinking in truly individual ways. It protects the herd and to a degree imprisons the individuals. It's not an organized plot – it doesn't have to be. It's the way we are. We are, for the most part, quite predictable, and so social pressure is quite enough to control us. Whether they exist or not, we don't need Illuminati or other secret overlords. We do it to ourselves. The only difference at all between this and the "peer pressure" we warn our children not to give in to, is immediacy. The kids want to *do something now,* and the adults want you to keep quiet, toe the mark, and have "good habits," whatever that means, but in the end it's all the same: peer pressure. After a while we fail to notice that it's even there. Even without an emperor, the Empire takes control, and we allow it.

I didn't notice the pressure from the kids, for the most part, and for the most part I also missed the background pressure from the adults. I'm largely immune to advertising and don't give a hoot (or any other part of an owl) what's popular or "in fashion." The announcement of The Empire's New Clothes never got to me, and I couldn't be happier.

The Empire expresses itself in the subtle peer pressure we face as adults, and as the overt kind we faced as children. It's really about doing what you think your neighbors think their neighbors think you should do. Be wary of that! I remember a poll in the years before Internet porn that asked people two questions about TV programming: would you rather see more sex or more violence, and which of these would your neighbor prefer. By a two to one margin, people asked for more sex – but when asked what their neighbors would rather see, *violence* won by that same two to one margin! What we think is expected, often isn't! People wanted to see this Emperor without clothes, but they believed they were alone in that. I think TV has adapted to that, but I don't think that people's expectations of other people's expectations have.

Perhaps the Internet has helped with that a bit. People do get to see more of what other people are *actually* doing and thinking, and they find groups of people – even if scattered across the globe – of like mind. They still worry about it, but at least they get to pick their "neighbors."

Pathology

I see most people as pathologically hypersocial. They go out in crowds and call or text other people at the same time. They go crazy if left alone, as if the most frightening thing there, is yourself. They won't go to a movie, or to dinner, or out in public at all if they don't have someone with them. How's that again? They won't go into places where there are people, unless they bring one with them!

"It's really crowded there this time of day, so I'd better bring even more people and make it even worse!"

People worry about what others might think about what they're doing. They don't trust their own experiences and judgment until they find that others agree with them. Psychologists call this "validation," as if our observations are somehow invalid until we find someone who agrees with us. No wonder original ideas come out so rarely: no one wants to be alone, and if no one follows where they go they will be. So fear of being alone creates fear of being first, and their original ideas die with them. Also, no one else wants to go where only one person is. It's a self-fulfilling prophesy of ostracizing. Who really makes the leader great? The first follower. Once there's a follower who will proudly follow, then others will follow them.

If my ideas work, I don't care if anyone agrees with them so long as no one can disprove them. If someone – or some new fact – comes along and disproves my idea, then so be it. I'll find new ideas that work. If I were to wait for others to agree with me before saying something, I'd never have published this book! I don't really even care if you agree with any of my ideas, as long as they make you think. If as you read my ideas you come up with your own ideas that work better for you, then I've still helped and that's terrific. I've done my job.

For good and bad, the people who change the Empire the most are the ones who don't care what it says about them. Social liberalization makes a lot of old Imperials nervous. They want the Empire to stay as it is because they understand it and they're comfortable thinking that they know how people will act. They live in "tight" cultures where any deviation from an extensive and intricate set of oft-unspoken rules is met with punishment. Social liberalization frightens these people, and it does something else: it advances technology. By taking the binders off of what people can do and leaving the Empire only to mediate disputes and limit any one group's power over others, social liberalization creates whole new opportunities for services and technology. It's good for business. Many European countries are getting good at this while being derided for it at a cultural level by the American South and Midwest. In America the research universities and "left coast" are rightly famous for it – and are making a good living at it.

The flip side is that being deeply immersed in your Empire is good for business, too, but in a very different way. Businesses in rural areas occupy smaller niches, employ fewer people each, and are far less "disruptive." They're more locally-connected, more personal, tied to very local needs, and reflect the growing reality: if you want a rural job, you've got to make it yourself. Nearly a quarter of rural people are self-employed, and only a sixth of those are farmers. I don't think that "live-anywhere" consultants and salesmen make up a majority of the rest. Not by a long shot, but they do get the attention of the rural folks I've had the pleasure of living around, and they are part of the perceived threat to the rural lifestyle.

Rural business may not be as exciting as the big-city startup culture, but its rewards are often deeper and more personal, and ironically it's more stable. In my experience it's harder to get started there if you're a newcomer. Trust there is something that grows with generations of familiarity. If your grandparents weren't born there, it'll take people a while to warm up to you. For better and worse, tech startups lack that.

What Is a Culture?

Some say that a culture is just the sum of the decisions of individuals, and that's true to a point, but you have to also recognize that social inertia holds as much sway over the decisions of those individuals as their own perceptions do. People do or don't do because it's what they believe that other people expect, and they aren't even aware of it most of the time. From that mixture of inertia and initiative it's possible to understand people, so long as we can tell when they're acting on one or the other, and that's hard enough to tell for yourself. That internal stress has to release somehow. If you don't care about the Empire then you're a rude, arrogant bass turd. If you do, then you're under stress from conflicting inputs. Loud people rail against this stress often, while quiet people tend to be afraid to talk about it so they keep it contained. I think that's why the quiet ones snap in a big way while the loud ones just get into a lot of little trouble. Take your pick: a lot of small tremors or one big nine pointer. I try to keep my cool most of the time and make sure I have a very unconventional release when needed. I have some interesting stories from that.[4]

---

4   No lawyers were harmed in the making of those stories.

Most people do what's expected, but pretty often what's expected is just following unwritten rules, going with the flow, giving in to a kind of social inertia that pushes us along. But what is it we're really giving in to when we act "as we're expected?" Most people think that that means doing what others think you should do. As if that weren't enough of a constraint by itself, what those people think you should do is formed by what they think other people think, and so on. So when you do something to fit in, you're not doing what you think you should do, or what other people think you should do, but what you think other people think that other people think you should do.

Most people tell you that that's a good thing. I missed that announcement. I think it's horrible, though in the days when everyone knew each other and knew how much they all depended upon each other, it did help keep the psychopathic 1% in line. As society has gotten more complex that control has loosened because our interdependence is less direct. We don't know and never see the people we depend upon, and people are deluded into thinking they're independent. Really? Don't need the outside world? When's the last time you mined iron and made steel that you used to build an engine that ran on the gasoline you refined after getting the crude oil out of the ground? Surprise: you depend on millions of people in the outside world. Whether it's a generator, vehicle, chainsaw, or something completely different, you depend on a lot of people to make it possible. You may as well just accept that fact and realize that all those people making all those tools that you don't have to make, but that make your life go more smoothly, are doing you a great service.

Heyoka

In Lakota culture I found the concept of the Heyoka. The Heyoka is a kind of sacred clown: a contrarian, jester, and satirist, who speaks, moves and reacts in an opposite fashion to the people around them. Heyoka may weep when the people celebrate, rejoice when the people mourn, and even dance while the people starve. They live lives that are in most ways backward from the others.

13

THE EMPIRE HAS NO CLOTHES!

Heyoka can say things and ask questions that others fear to ponder. Unbound by social constraints, they challenge the social codes that bind others. They may wear their clothes inside-out, arrive naked at formal gatherings, or simply run around flattening things that should be round. They ease the shame of others by gleefully and openly singing or acting out their own shame. We all make mistakes and find ourselves in conditions that our culture tells us are shameful, yet if we've acted well and merely failed, that's not shameful but grand! Let's celebrate! I'll put a scoop of rocky road ice cream on top of my hat and dance with you in celebration until it melts.

This concept doesn't translate to modern western cultures. People who do this are regarded as insane at worst, more likely as antisocial and possibly dangerous, or callous and uncaring at least. We are only beginning, in the digital age, to accept the role of the "disruptors" as we call them, and even then only in business but not in society. The Empire is split on this one. Disruptors are scary, but too profitable to ignore.

I haven't had visions of the thunder beings of the west, and no one who has the right to do so has ever granted me the title of Heyoka; but being as I am, and seeing things very differently as I do, I relate strongly with this idea. To put it in western terms, as one friend of mine did, I "not only don't think inside the box, [I'm] not even in the same warehouse." It's taken me a rather long part of my life to even begin to recognize the myriad boxes people use to compartmentalize their thoughts. It's kind of complicated, but I get it. For me the only compartment I seem to have is "what I need," and that's a box that's hard to think about because it doesn't really affect the rest of the universe. It's first and foremost for most people, but for me it rarely makes itself known. I'm just an agent of the universe, so what I want has been of little concern for most of my life[5]. I'm only one of billions of people, and we're likely only one of billions of sapient races in the universe. In that way I'm not much, and that's okay because I'm made of

---

5   My family's needs, on the other hand, are pretty important to me. There are more of them than there are of me, so they're easier to think about. I've finally realized that to take care of them I have to take care of me. I actually do have a duty to myself. Weird.

14

the same stuff that everything is, and "everything" is full of amazing stuff so I am too!

Like the Heyoka, I break social norms and use humor to point out how silly they are. When someone says, "guess what I found," I'm likely to guess a purple rhinoceros under their bed, maybe with a scoop of that same rocky road ice cream in each ear! They don't actually want me to guess, but they tell me to, so I do. Sometimes, when people are celebrating an accomplishment this way, I make a guess so absurd that it couldn't possibly be relevant. Sometimes they take me seriously and the end is an offense taken. It's frustrating for both of us, but this is how I am. *Don't ask any question you aren't ready to receive an answer to!*

I'm Backward!

My whole life has been backward. When the economy is down, I'm getting the best work of my life; and when it's up, I'm unemployed. That hasn't worked out so well for me. On the other hand, I've been pretty happy even when most around me have been miserable, and when I'm miserable most others are happy, so the pains shared are pains divided and joys shared are joys multiplied, so that's worked out very well, indeed. Now, as I approach that later part of my career where most men have made their fortunes and are seeking something meaningful, I've had a very meaningful and rewarding career and now I'm finally looking at trying to make more money in addition to just trying to make a difference. Sometimes you can do both, and I hope this book might just manage it. I've been working on it in various forms on and off for close to 30 years, so even a little compensation for all that effort is nice. Thank you!

I'm taking on some very serious subjects, even some that most people won't talk about, and trying to help us think and maybe laugh about them when others just get angry for raising the question. Maybe I can help you see the world through my eyes. Well, not actually, because I'd really like to keep my eyes. I'm kind of attached to them. Use your own!

15

It's About Agency

No, not the Central Intelligence Agency, or "have your agency call my agency." It's a different kind of agency. Your free will, if you will. Self-determination. Power. Your ability to understand your own options, make your own decisions, and act upon them and is called agency: being the agent of your own fate. To have agency you need information, rights, and resources. Information gives you choices, and rights and resources give you the power to do something about them. Just having choices doesn't give you agency if you don't have the resources to exercise those choices. It comes in degrees, and you don't have to be able to do anything you might possibly want on a whim. You do have to have the power to make and exercise decisions that affect your life and the lives of others in your care.

The Root of All Power

You need information to know what your situation is and what all your options are. You need to know the risk and benefit exposures of each possible course. That's a lot of information. Without it, the others mean nothing.

What we think of as power is usually the ability to express our own agency over that of others. To make others do what we want. The only real power we truly need, though, is to express our own agency: to do what we want to do without impacting the agency of others.

16

You also need to know who else will be exposed to the risks and benefits. For them to exercise their own agency, they have to be brought in to the decision-making process. That's where it gets complex, because your agency affects the agency of others, and theirs affects yours.

After information you need rights. Without the right to take an action, well, what good is thinking up a cool idea if you're not allowed to do anything about it?

Finally, you need resources. Every action takes energy and time, and most also need material and tools. Most of those can be traded for the other resource: money. If others like the idea you may be able to trade their money for the resources you need, in exchange for more money later. Begin to see how important money is to personal freedom in a capitalist society, and how the lack of it makes everything harder?

If you can't fail you can't try, and if you can't try you can't succeed, but what if your family will become homeless if you fail? Very, very few people will find the power to try under those conditions, and the ones who do try know that in addition to bearing responsibility they'll be vilified for any failure. The rest of us have it much, much easier.

Specialization

We live in a complex world where people specialize in one skill or another, and few master more than a handful. That makes each of us dependent on a host of other people to create, maintain, and drive the society and technology we depend upon.

This is where it gets weird. See, while my agency and yours can get in each other's way, and being dependent on people often means you have to bend to their schedule, dependence on the "outside world" doesn't decrease your agency at all! It multiplies it by giving you lots more choices about what you do to survive. We don't all have to hunt, farm, and fight off predators any more. We can write computer programs or books, build cars or houses, paint, write poetry, run a shop, play sports, invent things, design weapons or clothes or spacecraft, the list is

17

amazingly long! We have choices.[6]

That dependence is more anonymous than it used to be. Long ago, if you cheated your tribe everyone knew it was you and you were likely to die, so you didn't. Then came a time, exemplified by the wild west, when the agency brought by new technology like repeating arms and steam trains met with vast open lands, small towns, limited communication and law enforcement, and relatively swift transportation for free agents. Many Americans think that that was some kind of normal thing in human history. It wasn't. It was a high point for the agency of a few and the lasting fantasy of many, but it was short-lived. It's been said that the actual wild west era contained fewer minutes than all the western movies put together. It would take about 4,500 movies to fill a year. The wild west was just short of twenty. Are there really 90,000 westerns? That might be fun, but even if not it does help to make the point that that era was short. I also don't think there were nearly so many murders in that reality as in the westerns we do have.

One Universal Right

Parts of the Empire tells us that there are a litany of things that are always right. Other parts try to convince us there are no absolutes, CIA nothing is always right. To me, again, they're both wrong. The one thing I see as always being right is to find out what things people want (that aren't wrong) and help them with that.

I don't get to decide what's right for you. It's important because something that works for me might not work for you or anyone else. Too many people are the head pastor of the First Church of Me. They never realize that there's a lot of their own personal history and nature that come together to make something work for them. Everything works at least a little differently for everyone because we're all so different

---

6 Don't get me wrong, making a living isn't easy. Since the dawn of agriculture and maybe before it never has been, but thanks to having so many options it's slowly getting easier – and rapidly more complicated. Many professions are getting harder to get into and out of, and others are getting easier to make a living at. It's a mad, mad, mad, mad economy.

ourselves. What we want and why we want it, and how we think about how to get it, well, no two people are completely alike even if some are very close. I've come to realize that the life we want to live is mostly determined by how we define and understand our own agency.

I don't make your decisions and you don't make mine. It's a relief that I don't make yours. Mine are hard enough, thanks! When one group tries to make decisions for another, and the other group doesn't like it, we get war. In the 1990s TV series "Babylon 5," (you should look it up) Ambassador G'Kar makes an impassioned speech to the representative of the people who had just conquered them in war. He says,

> *"No dictator, no invader can hold an imprisoned population by force of arms forever. There is no greater power in the universe than the need for freedom. Against that power tyrants and dictators cannot stand. The Centauri learned that lesson once. We will teach it to them again. Though it take a thousand years, we will be free."*

I couldn't say that better myself so I'll just shut up now.

Not really, but I won't try to outdo G'Kar. How people define freedom – and oppression – depends greatly on how they define and practice their own agency. When you understand that about someone, you can then understand the life they want to live, and from that you will know why they believe what they do. If you meet someone whose sense of agency has crumbled, then you have met someone in desperation. Someone on the edge of violence. The way to help is to understand how that sense of agency can be restored. When you know what makes someone feel powerful and help them achieve it without harming others along the way, then you've saved someone – and maybe many.

I Don't Need Other People

Actually you do. Coming back to an earlier point, other people having power over their own lives helps you, even if you don't ever see

19

them. By letting them do the work they enjoy[7], it keeps you from having to do things you don't or can't. I can't refine gasoline. I can't mine iron or build engines or do the kind of lithography that makes a hundred million transistors at a shot. There are a lot of things I can't do, but that I can't live my life my way if they aren't done. I need computers, and the things designed on computers. I need gas engines and gasoline and sharp cutting tools and heat and light. I don't have to waste my time making those things, so I get to spend my time doing other things. Mostly I program the computers whose processors I can barely fathom any more[8]. I use computers to design things in the hope that those things will save me money, or make me some, or help me live the life I want. If you live in Alaska, or the African bush, or the Outback of Australia, or the Himalayas, at some point you depend on supplies brought in by airplanes. And you need all the people in all the parts of the outside world that go into making the tools and parts that make that airplane. Other people, doing their thing make your life what it is. Other people exercising their agency make yours greater.

How Do I Get It?

The first thing you need to have agency is information. It has to be correct information. If people are lying to you then they're keeping you down. In normal life it's *never* okay to lie.

So you need accurate information. You also need *all* of the relevant information. Every possible risk and every possible gain. Everyone who might be affected, and how. And on and on. Never stop getting information. Agency is power, and information is the first necessary part of agency. Information is power.

Guess what! This means that no one has the right to lie to you. It also means you don't have the right to lie to anyone else.

---

7 We hope! Or at least doing work they're good at. We hope.

8 Sure, I can still program them and know the machine code and timing diagrams, but with multiple cores and pipelining the actual circuitry isn't something I can just see in my head like it used to be. A hundred million transistors are too many.

I said its never okay to lie. Well, almost never. If it's the only way to achieve the highest sum, and no one is harmed or put at any kind of risk, and the outcome benefits people other than yourself, then it might be okay. Keeping the secret that you're really taking your friend to a surprise party that you know in advance they won't mind (some people hate surprise parties) is a good example. If you want to do that for me, I'm game. Lying to a thief about your passwords or PINs is another. Lying to get someone into an investment that you need to go up is not, no matter how much you believe in it. Situations where lying is okay are incredibly rare. I can count the ones in my life without getting above two. If your count is too high to count, it's a failure of imagination on your part. Look for better answers. Look hard.

The Good and the Bad of It

Some people measure their power, the degree of their agency, by how many people they can help. These people are good to have around.

Some people measure it the opposite way: by how many people they can inconvenience. They purposely walk slowly in front of traffic or crowds, argue with retailers, and slow down things at work with needless complications. These people suck. They're not just pitiful, they're bad people. They make the lives of others worse just to satisfy themselves.

Find your power by helping others. Do that, and it's perfectly alright to help yourself along the way, and have those others help you in return. That's how good businesses are built and run. They aren't all that way.

What We Believe

Why We Do the Things We Do

The Empire tells us that what we believe determines how we act, and how we live our lives. That's true, but it's only part of the story. Where, after all, do we get our beliefs? We get a selection of beliefs presented to us, selected for appropriateness by the Empire. They come from our family, our church, our local culture, and the myths (some factual, some not) that our larger culture believes about itself. The Empire would have us believe that they are the beginning of our motivation. From what I've seen, it's the not our beliefs that give life to our motivation, but our motivations that give life to our beliefs. *The life we want to live determines what we believe*, and those beliefs and motivations get locked in a dance where each informs and drives the other. Sometimes this Emperor has clothes, but most times not. The Empire has only part of the story, and it's used beliefs and peer pressure to keep people toeing that line for thousands of years – to confine their motivations.

When we find that we've been misled, or that our beliefs have been holding us back or don't support our motivations, more often than not we keep our motives and change, reinterpret, or ignore our beliefs. Sometimes only then do our deepest motives find a voice, for better or for worse.

Many followers of many religions do good works and go to great lengths to help others in the names of their gods and faiths, and that's wonderful. We are all better for it. There have always been some others, though, who use their religion or other beliefs to care only for themselves or as an excuse to harm others. "God's people will not be found begging bread" is used as a validation of greed, and "it's harder for a rope to pass through the eye of a needle than for a rich man to find the kingdom of Heaven" and "the love of money is the root of all evil" are ignored. They pick and choose the verses that reinforce what they already believe, and they believe as they do because of how they want to be. Jesus's words, "I did not come to bring peace, but a sword," and similar verses in the Koran and other holy texts, are used to validate the desires of people with violent dispositions. Never mind that each passage must be taken in proper context to be understood. People use their own confirmation bias to accept ideas or "facts" (genuine or "alternative") simply because they agree with what they already believe, and reject or ignore those that don't. It's a dangerous thing and unlike The Force, it's strong in us.

Every day I hear people trying to use the self-espoused beliefs of politicians, pop stars, terrorists, or whomever else, in an attempt to understand the behavior of those people. I find it can't be done very often, but far more often what I can do is discover the world these people want to live in by examining the parts of their religion that they exercise and the parts that they ignore. Again, their beliefs don't regulate their actions but the life they want to life determines what they believe.

What do the parts of your belief system that you cling to, say about you? If you're not sure how to answer that, look at your actions to date and that should tell you a great deal about the life you want to live, and which parts you're really paying attention to. If you feel guilty about doing or not doing some of the other things, why doesn't that translate into action? Is it because you really don't want it to? Are you just feeling guilty out of peer pressure, and if the others weren't there to reinforce those social norms, would you even care?

THE EMPIRE HAS NO CLOTHES!

Diversity

We all come from different backgrounds, and we all have different predispositions. This makes for an infinite combination of histories, abilities, and so on. No two people will – or even CAN – respond exactly the same to the same situation, and much of that is beyond their control. "If I can do it, anyone can" is one of the most damaging delusions we have. You have talents, limitations, and predispositions, subtle or obvious, that make you uniquely suited to something. When you find that "niche" or "calling," don't assume that everyone else can do it. There's a very, very slim chance you might just be the best at it and a very good chance you're better than most.

Talent

I've known a lot of people who've said to me, "I don't have any special talents." When I point their talents out to them, they say, "That's not a talent. It's too easy – anyone could do it!"

A talent is anything that comes easily to you and not to others. Next time you notice you're doing something easy that most other people aren't doing, you might just have discovered that you have a talent. Make the most of it! Raise the sum! Play with it! Do what you love and you'll never work a day in your life. That's the agency that all those other people doing all those other jobs has bought you. Be grateful for that.

Be humbled by your talents. Other people have to get by without them, and look what they've achieved! Be proud of what you've *made* of your talents. Noblesse oblige: nobility obligates.

Chaos

Talents, limitiations, perspective, nature, and nurture: they all add up to you. There's a thing in mathematics called Chaos that kind of guarantees that no two of us ever end up exactly the same, or can even experience the same thing exactly the same way. Many of us got our introduction to Chaos from Jurassic Park, but we still don't really understand much of it. It's pretty simple, really, so if you'll let me be a bit boring for a while I'll walk you through it, starting with something warm and familiar.

Fire is an interesting beast – the heat released from one molecule can give enough energy to nearby molecules to get them to release their stored energy. We call that kind of thing a *chain reaction*, and it's what allows a fire to grow. Matter has stored the energy, and when there's enough energy stored in some form of matter we call it fuel. Under certain conditions the fuel releases its energy, and in so doing rearranges the molecules and even combines them or breaks them up. Most of the new molecules fly up into the sky and away, leaving relatively few behind as ash. The fire is a chain reaction that's made up of energy scattering matter and that matter releasing the energy it so carefully stored to scatter the matter... you get the idea. We know of nothing on Earth that's as good at collecting and storing energy as life is, so we find that energy stored by other once-living things in fossil fuels like coal and oil, and less ancient fuels like wood and grain alcohol.

All matter attracts other matter. Gravity isn't as strong as magnetism, after all a magnet the size of a quarter can lift something held down by the gravity of the entire planet, but it has an advantage: magnets work great up close, but gravity's range is unlimited. It's like the prom queen: given enough time it'll attract everything to itself. So a little hydrogen sticks together and becomes more hydrogen. "More" is more attractive than less, so the prom queen builds her entourage. After a while it gets crowded, then claustrophobic, then things heat up, and BANG! A Star Is Born. So astrophysics is a little like fame, at least up to there. A star is a big thing, and it attracts a lot of stuff, all going this way and that until it falls into some kind of random orbit around the star. Clumps gather together and eventually you have planets. Planets or fans clubs, it's all the same. Except a solar system is more organized than when it started and I have my doubts about fan clubs. Still, there are a few big things drawing a whole lot of stuff together into groups that are kind of all doing pretty much the same things in slightly different ways. From there you get fans making props and new fiction and other things and planets make complex chemistry and sometimes life. Life makes more life, which makes more life, and so on.

Everything is driven by the chaos of matter gathering together and energy going astray. Matter can bring energy together, just as the energy tries to scatter and take the matter with it. It's a dance where random energy, often carried around by matter, is attracted by forces that bring some order to the randomness. The asteroid belt is a good example. Millions or even billions of random-sized rocks moving at random speeds and random directions, drawn into an orbit around the Sun. As time goes on the asteroids collide and exchange energy, knocking the real oddballs out of the belt and averaging the rest out. We end up with a nearly perfect ring shape (called a "torus") made up of a disorderly mess. Up close it's madness, but from a distance it's a neat, clean shape. Gravity truly forges "one ring to rule them all."

The same sort of dance happens in your brain. The random firing of neurons causes a cascade effect like a great branching bolt of lightning that covers the sky. This random association is how we form ideas. But if the cascade were never to stop, as may be true in severe autism, we would never be able to focus on that idea or respond to a new stimulus. We would glaze over and rock our lives away in the infinite possibilities of our very first idea. For most of us, the cascade is interrupted. At some point, chemicals in the brain respond to the pattern and cause the cascade to slow down and eventually stop. Now we have an idea and we can focus on it. Without the randomness we could never have an idea. Without the order we could never focus on the idea and actually make use of it. Each of us strikes a unique balance between these. Most people who start companies (or countries) can't run them once they're established. It's a rare bird who can walk on both sides of the fence.

This dance is known as *chaos*, and the bits that bring order to it are known as *attractors*, like the gravity, the prom queen, or The One Ring. We don't have any choice about being in this dance, so we may as well have fun while we're here.

Business and technology are the essence of chaos. Millions of people try millions of new things every year. Less than one new business in ten survives. That's a lot of randomness going on! We try things, and the things that work not only stay and grow, but other people start to do them. Success of the idea is measured by growth. If it spreads, it succeeds. Successful ideas get more influential and unsuccessful ones wither and die. Business and technology *evolve* without anyone directing them. If it can be tried, it will be tried. That's good and bad, but it drives us headlong into no one knows what. No one can, because there's too much going on.

We don't need Illuminati controlling everything for the rush of change to be incomprehensible. There are seven billion of us each trying to change things. That leads us to yet another naked Emperor.

We are not in control.

With so many people making changes, and everyone else haphazardly deciding whether they like it for roughly 7 billion different sets of reasons, there's absolutely no way to predict in any detail what's going to come out next.

Malaria was once thought to be caused by wet, stagnant, tropical air. Air conditioning was invented to fight it long before the age of electricity. Would anyone have looked at that and predicted refrigerators, refrigerator magnets, liquid hydrogen rocket fuel, liquid oxygen for hospital assisted-breathing equipment, or freeze-dried instant coffee? Yet it all arose from a need to fight malaria and a completely wrong idea about what caused it.

Governments do, of right and with legitimate concern, try to exert some control to ensure that no one and no group of people, however large or powerful, just accidentally do something really, really bad – like killing every living thing on Earth. Don't think that's possible? Give a million kids with teen angst and severe boredom genetic engineering "Erector Sets" and see how that goes. By design or by accident, it won't be pretty. Just think what someone who hates everyone and is willing to die could do with it, and if we don't control that kind of power, they'll get it. Completely free, unregulated markets are like Sweeny Todd: a

THE EMPIRE HAS NO CLOTHES!

threat to everyone who just wants a nice shave and a haircut, and a false promise to everyone who just wants a tasty lunch at a reasonable price.

We are not in control. To a certain degree, we need to be. The discussion can't be about one extreme or the other, as it's been for the last few decades, but about *where the lines are drawn.*

Gifts From the Empire

Good Stuff

Not everything the Empire puts on you is wrong. After all, it's made us very successful. In just a few thousand years we've gone from a few million people to a few billion, from fire and stone tools to spacecraft and computers you can wear. The Empire exists because it's very good for the group. Sometimes what's good for the hive is also good for the bee, because what's bad for the hive is never good for the bee. That doesn't mean that being good for the Empire is always good for its subjects.

The Empire tells you many things that are good and right. It tells you that no one has the right to do wrong or prevent another from doing right, and that everyone should have the right to do right. It tells us that an act is wrong if it's harmful (murder) *or is intended to be harmful* (attempted murder).

The Empire has built a world where there's a place for every talent, so every talent can find a place. The problem is that navigating the Empire to find that place is a talent in itself and the Empire doesn't teach us that one. We would be a lot better off if it did, and it would, too.

The Empire gives you a framework for understanding right and wrong. It does it mostly through allegory, metaphor, myth, and force of law. By virtue of its human origin and maintenance that framework is

THE EMPIRE HAS NO CLOTHES!

flawed, but it's a good start.

The Empire gives us many forms of protection and all the infrastructure we need to develop and get cool new toys and tools. It then tries to tell us that we have to find a path to success, and that success can only be defined by the Empire's own rules. None of us who succeed by other rules are respected unless the Empire gets what *it* wants from us. The difference between eccentrics and lunatics is mostly in their value to the Empire. Other things being equal, If you try something wild and it works, you're an eccentric. If it fails you're a lunatic.

Finally, there's evidence that the Empire protects us from ourselves, then denies its own role in it. That can be good and bad, but one good example suggests that a lack of social connection – your "cage" – is a major, possibly root cause of addiction. People on drugs, even morphine, in hospitals almost never go looking for the stuff once they get out. In recent experiments, rats given good living spaces in contact with other rats wean themselves off the drugs they addicted themselves to when in cages. The chemical hooks we all know about may be part of the problem, but if only about 17% of smokers who want to quit can do so with nicotine patches, then a lot of addiction isn't well explained that way. Giving people a good social network and people to bond with often works better. Desperation does terrible things to people. Maybe even this. Helping them bond with people instead of chemicals may do more to cut demand for addictive drugs than anything else we can do. Take away the stigma and let the rest of the Empire do what it does best. It's worth a try.

Good Decisions, Bad Decisions

The Empire tells us that good decisions are those that turn out well, and bad decisions are those that don't. Rubbish.

If I risk everything I have on the Megaball, that's a bad decision[9]. I'm less likely to win that than I am to be hit by lightning twice in that same week. All I've done is throw everything I have, away. If, by some freak of chance, I actually win the jackpot, it doesn't suddenly become a good decision. It's just a bad decision that worked out well. Some people have been very lucky, and that by itself doesn't mean they've made good decisions.

On the other hand, along with having five fingers, I can do everything right and still fail. I can make a lot of good decisions, but if they turn out badly I'm still in trouble. I can do all the research, make the best plan, start a business, have good advertising and a good product at a good price, and still go bankrupt.

We can make good or bad decisions and succeed or fail – in any combination. Success and good decisions tend to go hand-in-hand, but it doesn't always go that way. Luck still plays a part.

---

9   Whether it's literally your house, your country, or all life; and whether you're literally gambling, testing out some new technology, or making nuclear weapons more accessible: *never take the deed to the house into the casino!*

THE EMPIRE HAS NO CLOTHES!

Risk Exposure

If ever there were a kind of exposure I'd call indecent, it's unnecessary risk exposure. "What is it," you ask. Good question. People who deal with risk all day, like insurance people, have this cool thing called Risk Exposure.

Suppose you had a choice between two actions with the same possible benefit. The first has a 90% chance that you lose $100. The other has a 2% chance of death. I know which one I'd take. The risk exposure of the first is 90% of $100, or $90. For the second, it's 2% of my remaining life expectancy, say, 50 years... so the risk exposure there is one year. Take my money.

Even a small risk of a catastrophic loss is far less acceptable than a large risk of a small loss. Hand a full genetic engineering laboratory to a kid with teen angst? With 7 billion people right now and maybe thousands of generations yet to come, the risk exposure for that is trillions of person-years. *Never take the deed to the house into the casino.* Did I say that already?

Playing: Winning, Succeeding, and Cheating

There Is a Difference

There's a difference between wanting to succeed and wanting to win. The great mathematician and "Beautiful Mind" John Nash taught us that. At least mathematically, everything we do can be thought about as a game (or the word "game" can be defined as something we do), and we can use that math to understand a lot about the things we do for love, money, power, or any other goal. He also taught us that there are three kinds of games.

Negative-Sum: where there's less when the game is over than there is when the game started. War is a negative-sum game. The way it's played is to destroy things and kill people in order to gain some advantage over them. I spent my time in the Marine Corps, and I can tell you that war is a horrible business. What Maj. Gen. Smedley Butler had to say about it some years after winning not one but two Congressional Medals of Honor, was the subject of his own book, *War is a Racket*.

Zero-Sum: where the amount of stuff is the same. Stock trading is a zero-sum game. I sell, you buy. Nothing was created or lost.

Positive-Sum: where there's more when the game is done than there was before. Manufacturing is a positive-sum game. Stuff is turned into better, more valuable stuff. Some sand is melted to glass, which is drawn thin and woven into fiberglass cloth, which is turned into a boat hull or airplane wing or a superslide.

A Positive Sum

Life overall is a positive-sum game. Look around. Were cities, cars, trucks, farm equipment, computers, toys, or anything else you use *anything at all* like they are now, 100 years ago? And with all that, there are billions more of us humans, too! Life is inherently positive-sum. We have 3-D movies, spacecraft, airplanes that can take us to the other side of the world, and computers and networks that can, to a degree, bring the other side of the world to us. It's amazing. Anyone who tells you that life is anything but a massively positive-sum game is either lying or blind. Or maybe they just want an excuse to act as if it were.

Quite a few sports, usually those with two teams or two people trying to keep the other from doing what they're attempting, are laid out as zero-sum games. Rugby, hockey, futbol (soccer), and football are all examples. In order to win you have to keep the other at bay. You can't just succeed on your own merits, you have to *stop* them in order to win. You have to *make them lose.* They're a lot of fun to watch, but a really crummy model for the rest of life. You don't have to win in order to succeed, and you definitely don't have to keep others down in order to succeed.

Nearly everything we do can be done better, with a higher sum than we achieve now. In business and in our personal lives we need to always try to find out how to best increase the sum without hurting anyone.

Everyone does best when each person does what's in the best interest of himself. That's also wrong. It's proved that we succeed best when everyone succeeds. Everyone does best when each person does what's in the best interest of himself *and the group.* Henry Ford understood this when he priced his cars affordably and paid his people so that they would be able to buy them. That's what got the ball rolling and replaced horses with "horseless carriages." He could have personally made a lot more on each car and kept his workers too poor to own them, but that wouldn't have sold nearly so many cars. Henry Ford made more money by charging less, when everyone around him warned him otherwise, and in so doing changed the world by bringing a new way of manufacturing to someone else's invention. Even though gasoline was hard to find initially, his cars ended up being cheaper than horses so more people could have transportation. Lower cost, better pay, more products sold, more jobs, and a higher sum for all.

Oh, and he invented the garage door. It seems he suddenly discovered that his first car was too big to get out of the barn where he'd built it so he cut out a section of wall and raised it overhead because it was too big to swing. No one saw *that* coming!

Playing To Win

That's how you play nice. Everybody should do that, but not everyone does. Some don't just play to succeed, they play to *win*, and with the idea of a winner there comes an idea of a loser. If you're playing with the goal of making others lose, if you choose the quick and easy path, as Vader did, you may win in the short run, but in the end you won't succeed as well. People will realize what you're doing and refuse to play. If you're so big that they can't avoid playing with you, then watch out! The pitchforks will be coming for you soon. People who lose their agency are slaves, and slaves eventually revolt because revolution is all they have.

If you want to keep on succeeding, make sure everyone around you succeeds, too. That way they won't need to revolt and they'll spend their success money making more success for everyone. Including you.

The way you win is by not playing to win, but to succeed.

35

Nobility and Honor, Good and Evil

There are a lot of ways people act. We can be good or bad, noble or evil. We can even be none of these things. We don't all seem to agree on what's good or bad, either. Surprise, surprise.

Results matter, but our intentions matter, too. Good intentions can't make a wrong right, but bad intentions can make a right wrong. No matter how much good you do, if you had set out to harm other people and merely failed, you were still wrong in taking the action. Attempted murder is still a crime.

Beyond Good and Evil

When we get down to right and wrong, we quickly get down to the matter of good and evil. You know, the fun parts. What makes someone good or bad, noble or evil? This is a case of something being so obvious we have trouble explaining it, so I propose the following definitions:

Nobility

seeks to improve the sum of life's game, without regard for its own gain and perhaps even at a loss to itself. It measures success purely by the good done for others. Mother Theresa was perhaps the most visible noble person in living memory. There are many examples, from heads of state to heads of homes.

Goodness

seeks to do right by finding very positive-sum games and playing fairly. The only thing separating the good from the noble is that goodness is still concerned with its own benefit as well. Nothing wrong with that.

Mediocrity

seeks to improve its own condition by playing the most positive game it thinks of at the moment, but that positive sum is restricted to the people initiating the game. Mediocrity probably doesn't even think about the effects its choices will have on others. It may do a great deal of harm, but almost always through negligence. A lack of attention, planning, and insight are the hallmarks of mediocrity. If it does good occasionally, it's rightly proud, but most such good is just as accidental as the harm it does. Mediocrity just can't understand why things don't turn out better.

Badness

seeks to improve its own condition by playing games of any sum, even barely-positive or less while unfairly increasing its own gain and reducing its own risk. Bad knows it's doing harm, but judges success only by its own gain. It has a severe negligence problem in that it never seeks to improve the sum for all. The victims of bad may sometimes benefit, but not nearly in proportion to the risks they may not have been told they were taking. Bad may (as in the case of many leaders of military coups) be acting out of a sense that it can "do things better" than everyone else but by acting in a fashion that increases the amount of harm (or decreases help) done, proves that it cannot. Bad, when it becomes too powerful or desperate, often turns evil.

Evil

seeks to improve its own condition (or achieve any other goal) by

37

whatever means are available and may even take pleasure in the losses of others. Evil knows the harm it's doing and may choose its actions or measure their success based as much upon how much others lose as upon how much it may gain. It often sees the two as one in the same. Unfortunately, evil rarely sees evil in the mirror and may mistake itself for nobility. No one else, however, has any trouble telling the difference. In short, evil cheats and may even seek out zero- or negative-sum games and then play to win.

A quick reading of this will lead some of you to the conclusion that a schoolyard bully is evil. You're right. A schoolyard bully steals, frightens, and does physical harm to his peers primarily for fun and to increase his own sense of self-worth. The bully hates anyone who tries to raise the sum for anyone except the bully, and blames everyone else when what goes around, comes around. A bully is evil, but is the most petty and pitiful kind of evil there is. There may be one in every class, but it's usually only one. A very small percentage.

Most of us, I think, have good motives but wander into mediocrity when it comes to planning and execution. We are mediocre at being good, and need to be more aware of side effects. We don't see far enough beyond ourselves. Remember what effect your own carelessness may cause a better person forced by circumstance to be the mechanism by which your mediocrity catches up with you. In other words, don't play on the freeway because you may ruin or even end the life of the person whose car kills you. That, in turn, may have horrible effects on the people around them. Playing in the freeway is stupid and you'll deserve the harm that comes to you, but does the driver who is unlucky enough to be there really deserve it too? Killing someone, even accidentally, is a horrible thing to live with and many people never recover. Some don't survive.

Noblesse Oblige

The old saying "nobility obligates" holds true, but bear in mind that what they called nobility back then we will call the ability to be noble (being the beneficiary of nobility also obligates, but we'll deal with that some other time). Not all so-called noblemen act with nobility. We should always seek the opportunity to be noble when it's within our power. The more power we accumulate, the more people we can reasonably help and the more responsibility we inherit. Yet many pretend that even with all the power in the world they can still act as they did before. It's clear that the more people my actions may affect, the more careful I have to be in considering the impact on all of them.

"When I was young I had all the choices in the world and no power at all. Now I have all the power in the world and no choices at all."

- Emperor Mollari, "Babylon 5"

But we do have choices, even then. One is to relinquish power, peacefully and gracefully, as is the custom throughout the democratic world. Eventually the weight of responsibility should encourage us to give up some of our power in exchange for freedom, as twice George Washington did two centuries ago. At the end of the American revolution, General George Washington addressed his weary and embittered troops. As is so often the case in times of armed revolt, the troops were months or even years behind in their pay and were understandably angry with the Congress. They were itching to march on Philadelphia to take by force what was rightfully theirs, but in so doing would have destroyed all they had suffered so greatly to gain. But General Washington came before them and, in an unprecedented show of physical weakness for a military officer, paused to withdraw his eyeglasses from his pocket and put them on.

"Excuse me," he said, "but I find that in addition to my years and my livelihood I have also given up my eyesight in the cause of freedom." There was not a dry eye in the house, and he had for the first time in human history prevented an armed revolution from turning into a military coup. Many years later, after serving two unsought terms as President, he again walked away from power he could easily have kept. No one before him had ever voluntarily given up so much power even once, but George Washington provided the greatest model of nobility by serving and then retiring, not once but twice. Yet so very few of us have the wisdom to find the balance. Perhaps it's because we never really think about it.

Getting it Right Every Time

Not going to happen. It just isn't. It's important to remember that goodness and nobility don't require perfection. Good and noble people make mistakes all the time, just like the rest of us. Those who do the most good have probably also done the most, and also made the most mistakes. It's true of people, societies, organizations, governments, and countries. Henry James said it well:

> *"Excellence does not require perfection."*

You can have so much power that wielding it works against you. Simply having so much more power than your neighbor makes you a de facto bully whenever you ask for something: the implied threat is there whether you mean to use it or not. It's not a good way to keep our friends. Kudos go to the government of South Africa, which cut up its small nuclear arsenal for this very reason. Were its reasons noble? No, it found that being the lone nuclear power on a politically unstable continent severely restricted its ability to engage in both negotiations and small border battles and increased the motivation of its unstable neighbors to be so armed. Still, it illustrates the point: power enhances freedom only to the point where it begins to limit choices. I'm a lot freer in many ways than the President, which is one reason most of us just don't want the job. Remember that the next time you are offered more power at work – power brings responsibility and responsibility is an obligation.

Cities, Towns, and Farms

"They just don't get it." - City people about country people.

"They just don't get it." - Country people about city people.

I've lived in some big cities. I find them a bit too crowded for my taste, but they sure do have a lot of stuff to do. There's only one city that I've ever loved, or even liked very much, and I live near it now. If I can ever afford to I'll move in. I recently lived on a 20-acre parcel three miles outside a town of hundreds. I really liked that, though the lack of nearby kids was hard on mine. Driving from that rural setting to my new urban one required driving across the rolling hills of Montana. You can stand atop one of those rolls and see a thousand just like it stretching as far as the horizon. You can go to that horizon and the view is exactly the same. You can repeat that for hundreds of miles in every direction. By the second day driving across that, we were changed in ways I can only describe as spiritual. I can only imagine what growing up and living your entire life there does to your view of the world. It's not the same world as anyone else's. It's not my rural Illinois life with my fifty foot waterfall and neighbors a thousand feet away, and it's not my city life with neighbors dozens of feet away. It's... endless.

High population density puts a different spin on sticking to the social rules. In small towns and rural areas any odd behavior is immediately known by everyone. In big cities it's a bit different because there's some anonymity, though technology is changing that, and the things that affect others are actually different.

THE EMPIRE HAS NO CLOTHES!

On my old 20-acre place I could crank up the stereo and walk my land in the nude and no one would see or hear. If I had a pile of debris in my yard, lit a bonfire, created a rainwater catchment, or shot targets with a bow or a gun, no one else was affected. In some directions the nearest people were a mile away. They probably couldn't even see what I had or was doing from the road – they could barely see my two-story house! Libertarian government works a lot better – and quite differently – when people are a little farther apart, even though it seems like it might be more important when they're close together. What your neighbors do 1,000 feet from you affects you less than what they do on the other side of a shared wall.

"Good fences make good neighbors," they say, but "fences" are very different in a downtown apartment tower. When people are that close together the rules about what's okay and what isn't, change. People's outlooks on life change, too. Our perspectives adapt to what we can and can't do in our own space. Even our definition of what is and isn't our own space changes. Even in town, in a single-family house you own both sides of the wall. These things have to change because there just isn't room to run barbed wire in an apartment – but meeting up with friends doesn't require advance planning and transportation, either! When your best friend is next door it's quite different from when you're three miles apart.

Policing is very different, too. With everything spread out so much, individuals are much more responsible for their own security. If you shoot at a burglar and miss, or you accidentally discharge a gun, well, in a farmhouse you're not likely to hit any of your neighbors; in an apartment building or zero lot line neighborhood that's a very different matter. Bullets penetrate half-inch drywall much more easily than they penetrate people. "Oops! Sorry!" isn't going to cut it. I've met someone who was shot through his apartment wall by a neighbor handing a gun he thought was unloaded to a friend. He lived, but he illustrates that the rules have to be different in the city because the odds are different. The rules for each are repugnant to a lot of people who live in the other place. Many big-city dwellers would never give up the city, and many country people would never set foot in one. One thing I know is that they don't understand each other at all, though as a rule, once it's explained to them, city people do seem to have an easier time understanding their distant rural heritage than country people do understanding the cities.

It seems to me that the places where one person's liberty come in conflict with another's decreases as the square of the distance. Twice as free needs four times the distance. Three times as free needs nine times the distance. When my nearest neighbor shared a wall I was far less free than when my neighbor's house was 12 feet from mine; and when my nearest neighbor was 600 feet away through the woods, it was like a whole other planet. So people in cities *have to be* more orderly, less affecting of others. Their idea of personal space becomes smaller. They become insulated from one another, more private, because who knows when you're going to run afoul of someone? When you run afoul of someone whose sense of agency is already threatened or gone, that person may become violent. Multiply that by ten thousand encounters a day with strangers and you begin to "get" city people. They're not afraid, but they do have some very different and very practical rules for interacting with the people around them that don't work in rural areas.

Compare that with a small town or farm community where everyone knows everyone else. They can help one another in times of trouble, because they *know* when there's trouble, often even if you don't tell them. Anything you do that does get noticed can affect your standing in the community, even your children's. The sins of the parents are visited upon the children, even if the "sin" is simply seeing things differently.

There's a lot of physical privacy in the country, but not any other kind. Everybody talks, and anything that gets out, everybody knows. In cities, that effect is diluted beyond the point where it matters. Both people value the kind of privacy they have, and care less for the other kind. That reflects in their politics.

My friend and fellow writer Martin L. Shoemaker once said, "the good things about a city can be visited. The good things about the country must be lived." I agreed with that for a long time, until after 20

43

years and a dozen cities I finally found a city that I loved. I was amazed that it happened. I never really even liked cities before. I loved my quiet, libertarian, somewhat isolated, rural life. I finally found a city that has the feel of a small town I loved in southern Ohio. I can truthfully say that some of its good things must be lived, too.

Rural people fear that the lives they've known for generations are going away, and they're right. Farming becomes ever more industrialized and capital-intensive. Giant million dollar combines let one farmer do the work that thousands used to do. Coal mining is dead, replaced by natural gas wells that are safer, cheaper, more profitable, and employ far fewer people. Coal isn't coming back, and it's not just for environmental reasons. Your old rural lifestyle *is* going away, and the sooner you realize that and find a way to make it both financially viable *and* interesting for your adventure-seeking kids, the better your chances are of retaining it. Many of the rural people I know now are high-tech workers, stock traders, cold-callers, phone support, and other people who can work from anywhere. They're looking for a quiet place to contrast with their fast-paced jobs. That's not the same rural life.

As for smaller cities, they used to be unique. They had character. They were so cool! I remember when my sister told me that they had to drive 90 miles to get to the nearest McDonald's. It was a big thing at Michigan Tech in the 70s: at once a point of pride and an excuse for a road trip. They were remote, isolated, different, and proud of it. Last time I was there, they had McDonald's, Subway, Burger King, Home Depot, and about every other major chain I could think of. Houghton was no longer much different from the rest of urban America. It seemed somehow less for its Borg-like assimilation into the collective.

That assimilation makes a lot of rural folk feel like they're being oppressed. The ways of cities are taking over. Emily's grandmother's corner restaurant is replaced with a Dairy Queen. We are under siege. Well, yes, you are, but not by me nor by our government. You're under siege by a set of corporate juggernauts in food service, building supplies, entertainment, and even real estate that have already assimilated every major city and are working their way into ever-smaller towns in search of growing their profits to satisfy their stockholders. You are besieged by Wall Street and your culture is falling fast. Hold fast to your local businesses! Small banks and other local businesses are a blessing, and there are many in rural areas. There's nothing like the service that you can only get when the proprietor knows you personally.

The differences are even more pronounced in Alaska, where even the Federal Aviation Regulations (FARs) are different. So many of the minimums that apply elsewhere end with "except in Alaska." If Alaskan bush pilots were held to the same limitations of weather and fuel, a lot of people would die. As a necessary result, Alaskan bush flying is far more dangerous than we'd accept in the developed world, but the pilots are willing to take that extra risk to do a job that matters in a place they love for people they care about.

Families

Families can be complicated. A lot of people who do bad – even illegal – things play the "family" card. "You have to protect me. Families stick together." Bullshit. Family members protect each other, sure, but if I had a family member who murdered someone I'd turn them in in a heartbeat. There are enough bad people in the world. I don't need to harbor one of them. Being family means I know you well enough to know whether you deserve the benefit of the doubt or are a lying box of rocks.

Fealty

Being family also means there's an oath of fealty. If I bail you out of a tough spot, you gain an obligation that I'm not allowed to hold over you to return the good deed or pay it forward. The duty is mutual. If I bail you out time and again and you never make anything of the sacrifice I make for you, I'm fully within my rights to say "no" the next time you come to me. I have obligations other than you, and I have to balance them. At the point where you make that impossible my duty to you is more than fulfilled.

Babies, Children, and Parents

The Empire lied to me about children. Well, actually it understated its case to such a degree that it may as well have. "Everyone" told me

46

that having a child would "totally change my life." That's wrong. Having a child removed the life I had had and replaced it with something completely unrecognizable. It quite reasonably changed my tolerance for risk: I could afford to miss a meal or six, but that tiny, developing mind could not. It also made me paranoid and irrational. Fortunately I saw that and got better, but people (in America at least) really do get insanely protective around their kids to the point that they invent risks to be afraid of and then fly off the handle about them!

Our family isn't complicated. It was never supposed to be. I was in my 30s, she was in her early 40s, and for nearly thirty years, six doctors had agreed that she'd never get pregnant, and if by some miracle she did she wouldn't stay that way for long. We discussed it before we ever got engaged.

The pregnancy was unexpected, difficult, and life-threatening. It did permanent injury. It wasn't a choice: it was hundreds of them on a daily basis. Every day was the decision: do we continue? We got the best medical advice available. Genetic screening for Down Syndrome (negative). Weekly and then twice weekly visits to the doctors. Weekly ultrasounds and non-stress tests. Gestational diabetes. It was dodgy, difficult, expensive, and at every turn it was a self-defense situation. It ended in the worst case of toxemia the hospital had ever seen and an unscheduled Cesarean at 34 weeks. As four doctors hurried to prep her, I was the one who noticed her blood pressure collapsing and sounded the alarm. Four doctors in the room and I had a hand in saving her life. It was that bad.

During that pregnancy I presented myself with a simple decision. I could sit back, as if at a distance, analyzing and consciously under-standing the development of a child; or, I could dive in, and more than just get involved, immerse myself in the experience of growing up. I opted for the latter, and it's paid off in spades. It's been a most amazing journey for me, and it's given us a bond unlike any other. Knowing what I know now, plus knowing who she was at every moment, was all the guidance I needed.

THE EMPIRE HAS NO CLOTHES!

I didn't raise her, I grew up with her - young enough to need and old enough to know how we would both be best served. Able to see the long view through the eyes of her immediate need. We weren't separate in those times. I wasn't just her father and I wasn't raising her. We were, in many ways, one person. I knew the joys of discovering colors and the tonality of music. She benefited from forty years of experience with long-term consequences.

Mother's job is to protect. Father's job is to let you make all the mistakes you can recover from. Mommy's job is the same as Daddy's job: to be there for you, with you, to know you and to see the world through your eyes as well as their own, and to help you gain that understanding more quickly than they did.[10]

When she was about three, the little one was playing in a playground. "We have to leave in ten minutes," I told her. Like many three year olds, she sat down and started to cry. I knelt in front of her to get her attention. "We have to go. We're leaving in ten minutes. Now you can spend those ten minutes miserable and crying or you can spend them playing and having fun. The choice is yours." She froze, blinked, sniffed... I could see her thinking it through. She got up and ran off to play, and when it came time to leave she wasn't happy about that but was happy to have had the time to play. The ten minute warning – EXACTLY ten minutes – became an important staple of our lives. She enforced it on us from time to time if we met friends five minutes in.

The little one turned 17 this year. She's her own harshest critic, yet she knows her own talents. She knows that her value lies in those talents, not in her shape or her looks (which she tends to with unique style for her own reasons) or in vying for the fickle attentions of the local Empire. She has so many interests that she still hasn't decided which to pursue professionally, yet has a plan to try her hand at several while living a grander life than her parents have so far. She knows that the nature of work is changing and sees herself in the world that's coming. She wants to help people and have fun doing it. I think we did alright.

---

10 The best book I can suggest is "Teach Your Child How to Think" by Edward De Bono.

It's not "detachment parenting" or "attachment parenting." It's not any style of parenting with a name.[11] It's just getting to know and understand them at a depth that no language I know can describe. It's being there, emotionally and practically, when needed. Sometimes it means helping, sharing your experience, teaching or sharing a skill; and sometimes "being there" for them means letting them do it themselves so they can proudly display the glory of their success or seek solace in failure.

Remember, if they can't fail they can't try; and if they can't try they can't succeed. Nothing and no one is perfect. They don't have to be, to be wonderful. Their victories are theirs. Their failures are theirs. The lion's share of the time your part in these should go unmentioned. You know, and they know. Revel in the wonder without taking it from them.

---

11 If I were to name it I'd call it "Immersion Parenting." Like immersion living.

Enlightened Self-Interest

The Marshall Plan

In the early 20th century, a lot of national rulers were getting mad at and afraid of each other. It wasn't a good scene. Then some sniper killed one of these leaders and his pregnant wife, and Europe exploded into war. By the end of the First World War, there was very little left of Europe and the world sank into an economic depression. To make matters worse, the victorious allies followed a policy of continuing the negative-sum game against Germany by levying crippling reparations bills requiring it to repay all damages to the entire world before it could keep a penny to rebuild itself. Germany had started the war and had been soundly defeated, but that wasn't enough. Many countries thought it had to be broken.

The problem with that way of thinking is that life is resilient and refuses to be kept down. A new leader arose who fueled the passions of many, and was empowered by their support and the weariness of many who just wanted to have an economy again. He vowed that Germany would never again be beaten down. He vowed to end the negative-sum game they had started and now were being forced to play at their own expense. He quit paying reparations, built up Germany's industry and economy, imprisoned and killed people of Jewish faith and seized their assets. It's easy to get rich by stealing, but eventually you run out of people to rob so he set about to steal the whole world. The result was the Second World War.

I'm not saying that Germany was justified in its role in starting the Second World War, but I am saying we can understand it. Had the allies ended the negative-sum game Germany started when they had the chance, perhaps the 1930s and 40s would have gone better and another world war might not have been seen as the only solution. More briefly, "never start a fight but always finish it." Unfortunately, the allies chose not to finish it at the Armistice. An important lesson.

After defeating Germany for a second time, the world decided that a new approach was in order. Abraham Lincoln had long ago said, "I can destroy my enemy by making him my friend," and that's exactly what the Marshall Plan did. Rather than cripple a people already ravaged by war, America destroyed the government that started the war, tried and punished the war criminals, even its own, and rebuilt the economies of friend and foe alike.

The result has been more than seventy years of relative peace among the former enemies. Positive-sum games aren't always the easiest games to play. Sometimes they require great intelligence, wisdom, and planning. Sometimes corruption threatens to turn them into zero-sum games or worse, simply so some petty individuals can become rich at the cost of the lives of others. Played well, however, they're always better for everyone. Just make sure that when the stakes are high you have as impartial a referee as you can find.

World War is an object lesson in national agency. Beat another country down, verbally, economically, or militarily, at your peril. Better to help them find enough of their own power that they don't feel oppressed.

Helping Others to Help Yourself

Just like with the Marshall Plan, we can help ourselves by helping others in our everyday lives. Other people being powerful means they can do some things so we don't have to. Lifting others up is good for you. Give them power, help them define and apply their agency, and they'll be productive. When they're productive, that helps everyone. Making other people powerful makes you more powerful. Agency is like love: it's not a limited resource, everyone's better off when everyone has it, and making it is a lot of fun.

Globalism

This is a funny thing. It used to be the left that wanted globalism. They wanted an end to third-world poverty, and cheap goods. After all, there was enough wealth to go around. Done properly, there was, but no one was at the helm. It happened chaotically, piecemeal, as these things do. Then they noticed that a lot of their jobs went with it and they started shouting "bring jobs home!" About then the top 1% had come to like it because they could pay people less overseas and get richer. The right jumped on the bandwagon. Then they noticed the domestic economy was falling apart because so many jobs went overseas that fewer people were buying what they were making. The jobs weren't replaced by the "better" jobs they blindly expected, they were just disappearing. Neither saw the unintended consequences of their altruism or greed.[12]

Of course it was America, more than any other country, that would pay the price for globalism. We had the most, and so we had the most to lose. We paid for it over the course of my lifetime, from the 1970s through the 2010s. It's starting to pay off, just as politicians begin claiming the opposite. It would be a shame to "buy high and sell low" on this one. It's finally coming around as large parts of the former third world are about to become consumers of the stuff we do. And as they have more to lose and more agency they'll have less interest in war.

Why can't we all agree?

Because we can't. We can't even all agree that it's better to live than to die. If we could agree on that, suicide wouldn't be a word and we certainly wouldn't use it in relation to teenagers. If we can't agree on something that basic, how can we possibly hope to agree on anything

---

12 There was enough of each on all sides to go around.

else? Don't let that get you down, though. Most of us can agree on a lot. We need difference of opinion to keep us thinking. My pastor used to say that whenever two people agree completely on everything, one of them is unnecessary.

Privacy

Privacy is a strange thing in the Empire. We share enough information about our lives with enough people that we make it much easier to hurt us. Many of us don't fuss over handing over our Facebook profiles, pictures, posts, and even private messages in exchange for an "oil painting" filter of our profile picture. We hand our credit card or bank account numbers (ever write a check?[13]) to people we've never met. We do it every day and don't think about it at all. I do. I quit giving out my social security number when I was 18, a good 15 years before most others started thinking about it. Most of us will never have one check cost us thousands extra, but it can in the hands of a thief with the right skills.

There used to be a web site called "PleaseRobMe.com" that raised awareness of this. It scraped a bunch of social networking sites and could tell you how long a thief had to rob you while you were out. Back then, everything you put on Facebook or MySpace was public – there were no privacy settings. Only Google Plus had them. Things are better now, but far from perfect. Even your GPS can give you away. A burglar picks out a nice car, gets in, presses "home" on your GPS, and knows where your house is – and that you're at work. Security is getting better, but way too much is still hackable so be careful what you tell these machines. People are too clever for the rest of us to trust this

---

13 What's on a check? Your name, bank name, routing number, and account number. That's enough to electronically drain it dry.

completely. The defender has to be right, every time, in advance. The attacker only needs to be right once, and since the right breach could be worth millions, there are a lot of attackers out there.

Certainly, there are always going to be some things we don't want others to see. Even most of us who don't care who knows what about us, still care how those others find out. There are aspects of our lives we don't want misconstrued by the Empire. We want to control that narrative as much as we can. We want to be understood, so ironically we have to keep some secrets.

Yet while we hand out potentially compromising information all the time, we greatly value and protect our physical privacy, which is of no value to anyone. Sure, we want some control over the story of our lives, but how much harm does it actually do if your roommate's house guests accidentally see you naked as you go from the shower to your room? Why is this embarrassing, or for some even traumatic? For nearly all of us it's because the Empire tells you it should be, and *for no other reason.* We're all pretty much the same, physically, and I sincerely doubt you have anything I haven't seen before. It's not a big deal.

Little Things

Lots of Them

"When all is said and done, a lot more is said than done." The Empire calls this cynicism. I call it wonderful. If every fleeting, misguided statement by every person actually came true, I don't think there'd be a universe left to talk about. We are, for the most part, fairly wise, and we usually do weigh the good against the bad. We realize that a lot of the things that we've said shouldn't be done, and we don't do them.

•

The internet is an amazing thing. It shows us so many new places and opinions. We buy and sell, view art, and converse over it. Doctors assist other doctors. Pictures of cats. Political influence. So many things we do, we do better (and sometimes worse) and faster because of nuclear weapons.

Wait, what?

The Internet was created by ARPA (now DARPA), to protect computers from nuclear missiles. The only way, they reasoned, was to have the computer be in two different cities at the same time. So they invented the ARPANET to connect military computers (".mil"). One computer became a near-real-time copy of another, and they invented

56

email so the people using it could communicate. The civilians in the federal government wanted access to it (".gov"), and the contractors wanted it (".com").

Then it went public and the pictures of cats came. Them and a lot of really annoying people who want you to feel bad so they can feel good. That's all an internet troll is most of the time: someone whose sense of power comes from making other people feel bad. It's kind of pitiful.

•

Trolls or no trolls, don't be in such a hurry to feel bad! It may not be what you think! No point crying until you actually do prick your finger.

•

Efficiency is the art of enlightened laziness. Innovation is its primary tool. Things are rarely invented by people who set out to invent it. Most things are invented by someone who says, "there's got to be an easier way to do this."

•

If everyone were as bad at driving as most people think they are, no one would ever get anywhere. Out of the thousands of cars you interact with on a regular basis, it only takes one to make a mess of things. The vast majority of drivers you don't really notice because they're doing fine. The one or two who aren't, occupy your full attention. Much of life is like this. I guess life really *is* a highway!

•

Don't assume other people are in a hurry to feel bad! There's such a thing as being too sensitive. Don't take offense on behalf of someone who hasn't taken offense. You may not know everything that goes into that relationship. If you're that concerned, ask the person, "is that cool with you," and for crumbs' sake *accept their answer!* Just because you don't get it doesn't mean they don't. Don't forget the High Llama.

•

THE EMPIRE HAS NO CLOTHES!

Flip side: there is, and always has been, such a thing as being a jerk. Lazarus Long said that a skunk is better company than a man who prides himself on being 'frank.' An old friend of mine prided herself on being "brutally honest," but all she actually was, was judgmental and gleefully disparaging. She quit her job in journalism because the editor "only wanted the story, not the facts," then refused to hear my facts once she'd gotten enough story to attack with. She's no friend of mine any more.

•

People disagree a lot. When we're particularly unpleasant about it we have words for people who disagree with us. When we disagree about politics we may call each other unpatriotic at least and traitors at worst. When we disagree about sex we may call each other perverts. When we're a little more forgiving or disagree on just about anything else we may just call each other idiots.

It's time we learned again to disagree without being disagreeable.

•

Things will work out. Not because of any grand design for your personal life, or because of any great government or corporation (HA!) looking out for you. They only care about themselves and the Empire, not about individuals except as examples "good" or "bad" or in aggregate (I don't mean gravel, silly!). I say everything will work out because there are seven billion of us. If we hadn't found a way to make our world into a place where *things tend to work out for us*, there wouldn't be. I have seven billion reasons to be optimistic about my future. The cool thing is: things work out even better for optimistic people, and it doesn't matter why you're optimistic as long as you are. Believe that God, or your own wits, or random chance will get you out of this and it's far more likely to happen. Apparently when you don't believe you have a chance, you can't see the chances you have. Stay positive, my friends.

•

I'd be delighted if my wife made more than I do. I hate being the sole breadwinner because bearing all the responsibility for the health, welfare, education, and comfort of my entire family is more pressure than I want *or need* to bear. The load can be shared, and in sharing, increase my own agency. A complete safety net would mean I could leave a job I dislike, take only the jobs I would like, not have to worry about the 25% of my career when I'm between jobs... or maybe even go back to school and change careers entirely.

That the Empire says I have to was the first time I saw its clothes, and I hated them then. To my first girlfriend's mother: there is no "men's work" or "women's work." There's only the work that needs to be done and the person or persons best suited to do it at the moment. Very often that's just who happens to be in the right place at the time.

●

The dumbing down of America, and Western cultures in general, is a hot topic. It's not happening because of some nefarious plan, though there may be some nefarious plans to take advantage of it. It's because of the nature of advertising. Advertisers pay for news and other programming. They want their message to get out to the greatest number of people. Rare exceptions aside, if some people don't understand a show, they won't watch it. If they don't watch it, advertisers don't reach them. If advertisers won't reach them, they won't pay for it. If it doesn't get paid for it gets canceled. Advertisers are predominantly responsible for starting, funding, and driving the dumbing down of modern culture, even though it's not one of their goals *and may even be contrary to their best interests.* Every other influence is just along for the ride. Advertisers want the most reach for their money, so they tend not to support shows with a limited reach unless that limited reach is exactly their niche. It may be too late for broadcast television, though I am seeing some glimmers of hope. The Internet has made it possible to reach those niches cost-effectively, so maybe that trend will slow down now. Advertisers can now realize that being smart can be targeted, too. The dumbing down will continue in some channels, but it can be reversed in others. Each of us is a channel, and it's our responses to to what we see that ultimately drive it. Until we own that and really take control, it'll get ever-more-specific and the big picture will be lost in ever-more-narrowly targeted media for ever-more-narrowly targeted advertising. My one hope is that that can bring not just dumbing down, but more intelligent content to those who show an interest in it. The more we're all aware of it, all the time, the more we can make it better. Click smart, spend smart!

•

Dumbing down leads into the next thing: the reason and nature of media bias. The overall bias in the news isn't left or right, though there definitely is both. No one reporter, outlet, or agency can be completely unbiased. We're people, after all, and news outlets are paid by their advertisers who require them to attract a certain market demographic. That's a powerful Empire. We learn to understand and filter our friends' biases, and if we're paying attention we learn to understand and read through the Empire's biases as well.[14] After all, it gives us so many to choose from! There is an intentional bias in the news and it's been there since before the dawn of newspapers: "if it bleeds, it leads." News coverage has a sensationalist bias, and all the things that give me hope for the end of the dumbing down of everything, make me sad for the ever-accelerating growth of sensationalism. In an ever-more-fragmented media landscape, the news gets more sensational with every turn, just to try to get your attention. The quality of headlines is getting terrible.

It's not a conspiracy, just a perfect storm. Fighting it is up to each of us, to all of us. It's up to you. We need to be ever smarter, ever more aware, and there's reason to be hopeful about that. Another chapter is about why.

If you think that perfect storm has hold on us now, *and it does,* wait to see what it does to us when augmented reality and direct interfaces from the brain to the internet begin to control not only what we read but what we actually see and hear in the world around us! The promise of such technology is astounding, but if we don't fix that perfect storm before we

---

14 Penn & Teller and the University of Washington have both done good programs on this, both with "bullshit" in their titles. I'm sure there are others, but these two would be good places to start learning more about how our own biases are manipulated.

get there, we're in a lot of trouble. We need to start now. We can start by subscribing to multiple news outlets (to balance out the other biases) that take less advertising and shout less. Subscriptions equal security, and insecurity increases shouting.

Since 1993 violence is down, crime is down, murder is down,[15] all sharply, yet reporting on all of these is up. It would be nice to be able to look at the news and have some sense of our progress, some sense of where we are rather than where an ever-shrinking sliver of us remain. Sure, we need to know these things, and we still have a long way to go, but some balance would be good. Maybe some clever person can find a way to make it pay. Of course, anyone who tries will need our help.

NBC Nightly News, for example, does a recurring segment called "what works." It's a good-news piece on stuff that normally wouldn't make the cut. A good start, and it's been on a long time. Let's add to that and quit the dredging up of the worst people we can find to interview just to get people angry.

●

We've become pathologically risk-averse. We want guarantees that what we do will succeed. Well, there aren't any. A lot of that aversion comes from thirty years of stagnant or falling wages in real terms. If we fail, our children starve. Most of us have a lot less financial agency than we once did. Combine that with the fact that we're so afraid of the social stigma of failure ("he let his own egotistical dreams hurt his children – and for what!") that most of us don't try. Never mind that if that attempt had succeeded we'd be lauded as heroes. There's little the Empire abhors more than failure. Bad Empire! Go sit in the corner. No doggy treats.

Through the pressure to be perfect, or at least to never fail, the Empire forbids most of us to try. The truth is that most tries do fail, and to succeed you have to try. If you can't fail then you can't try, and if you

---

15 Recently cited increases are extremely localized and undoubtedly have specific causes but are nothing but outliers at this point. The trend is still down.

can't try you can't succeed.[16]

The beauty of modern software and prototyping (CNC mills, 3D printers, etc.) is you don't need a lot of cash to develop it. All you need is a computer that you probably already own, some open-source tools, drive, talent, spare time and energy, and an insight. It's still a lot, and lots of people will never have all those things at the same time, but at least you don't need to throw piles of money at it, too. You can try things without betting the farm, and when it's mostly working you can crowd-fund it. The later Gen-Xers and the Millennials invented most of this. Mostly unleaded entrepreneurs reinventing entrepreneurship and the world like their unleaded ancestors before them.[17]

Inventing some things is a lot less risky than it was even ten years ago, and it's just getting better. Of course, that means that a lot more people can do it, so you need to move faster. That great idea you have? GET ON IT! Before someone else does. That reminds me...

My dad and I sat in a restaurant one day at the end of a camping trip. He commented, as he often did, on how those coffee makers made such good coffee. I asked why they didn't make smaller ones for home use.

He replied, "there's no market for it, I guess."

I was a little confused, because it seemed I was sitting right next to the market for it. Late the next year, Mister Coffee came on big. Don't let anyone tell you that the world doesn't want your idea. They don't know any better than you do. Try it!

•

The measure of a society isn't its outliers. It's not how many millionaires is creates, nor how poor its poorest are, though both of those do tell part of the story. The real measure of a society is the

---

16 Pragmatism is a school of thought that focuses only on results: if something succeeds then it was good, and if it fails then it was bad. You set out to do horrible things, and through your ineptitude failed and somehow prevented a lesser evil so you're good. I find that appalling. Bad intentions matter.
17 More on unleadedness in a later chapter.

percentage of its people have real agency over their lives – and the percentage of those who don't. In America the number that do is smaller than anyone wants to believe or wants you to believe, and it looks to me like it's falling fast right along with real income.

•

When you shop only on price, you shop against domestic jobs – and eventually your own.

•

Government can't run like a business. It has to operate police, infrastructure, defense, air traffic control, and other programs regardless of the whims of the market or whether they're profitable. They need to be generally in proportion to the need, not in proportion to what "the market will bear." Privatizing Air Traffic Control might seem like a lovely idea until you realize that at some point staff will be cut *just to prop up the company's stock price.* Jeopardizing the public safety that way is nothing less than murder for hire.

•

Speaking of murder, there's a difference between *life* and *a life*. If I cut off my finger and toss it in a fire, in addition to probably being quite stupid, I've killed life. A billion cells in that finger were alive and I've killed them, but I haven't killed *a life*. It's dismemberment, not murder. The difference here is that there aren't any fingers out there living in their own tiny little apartments.

If I swerve to kill a squirrel with my car, I have intentionally killed *a life*. There are lots of squirrels out their living on their own in, well, okay: not exactly tiny little apartments. Still, it's not murder. The squirrel is a life but it's not a human life.

The political question of "when does life begin" is the wrong question. The right question is, "when does *a human life* begin." It's a very different question and it's another book.

•

THE EMPIRE HAS NO CLOTHES!

"Law-abiding gun owners don't kill people." That's utterly meaningless, because as soon as that previously lifelong, law-abiding citizen DOES kill someone they cease to be law-abiding and the statement no longer applies to them. What the statement is, is one example of what it is to be law-abiding. It's not a statement about the character of a certain group of people, regardless of what the Empire would have us believe otherwise. It's called a tautology and it tells you nothing except about the person saying it. "Except for my hair I'm completely bald" is another such statement and it means just as much.

•

Any plan that just needs everyone to [whatever] will fail. Whether it's perception, understanding, or behavior, everyone will never anything.

•

In the Cold War arms race, America didn't spend the Soviet Union into oblivion, but we did almost (?) do it to ourselves. The Soviet Union was doomed before Reagan was ever elected. No empire has ever survived more than about a decade of failure to provide its people with basic cereal. The day the Soviet Union started buying American grain to fill its own shortfall, its fate was sealed. About a decade later it fell.

•

Technology is a strange thing. The practice of it is even stranger.

When I was in college in the early 1980s I noticed that computer programs, especially those written in COBOL (a billion lines of it even back then), tended to be written to store dates with two-digit years. I told my professors that that was going to be a big problem and we'd all better get on it. They assured me that every program was modified every 9 months or so, so there'd be plenty of time. I didn't see that as a solution but a problem, because while all that changing is going on they'd also have to all be changed *at the same time* to fix the problem. After all, they all used the same files, and if you change the file format... Needless to say, when everyone panicked a decade later about Y2K, I wasn't sympathetic.

Twenty years later there was a debate going on in IT: did efficient algorithms still matter? An observation of mine was published in the Jan 24, 2004 issue of The Harrow Technology Report.

"In a similar vein, regarding growing processor performance, reader Grieg Pedersen reminds us that there's more to overall "computing capability" then just the speed of the processor: "I've never seen [the tongue-in-cheek] "Gates' Law" ["The speed of software halves every 18 months."], but I have had one distinct understanding from Moore's Law: if processor speed doubles every 18 months and accessible memory size doubles every 16 months (it was 2 years and 18 months, respectively, when I realized this), then processor response time is SLOWING exponentially, proving the need for multiple processors, specialty processors and improved algorithms. Add to this the fact that memory speed is not keeping pace with processor speed and you have a real problem. One need only work with image processing software like Photoshop or The GIMP to see how long response times can be."

I never heard anyone argue that algorithms didn't matter after that.

Now, of course, algorithms are all the rage, the very future of the industry; and efficiency, under the new and slightly broader moniker of "scalability" is on everyone's minds.

•

I'm a software engineer and craftsman by trade. In my business it becomes very obvious that *why is the beginning of what.* You can't know what to do until you understand why, and once you know why, the what comes easily. That what then becomes the why of yet other decisions, and so on until the cascade is complete.

•

In my father's day, shopkeepers paid people to walk around wearing sandwich boards. Today we pay the advertiser for the privilege of wearing logo clothes and we feel good about it. I don't get it. Stockholm Syndrome?

•

THE EMPIRE HAS NO CLOTHES!

Pronoun Trouble

In third grade, I think it was, the teacher told us that "when you don't know if the subject is male of female, the rule is to use the pronoun 'he' because it's assumed a man did it." In that very moment I decided the teacher was wrong about that. After all, half of all people are women so they must do about half of the things. When I read a female pronoun I know the subject is female, but when I read a male pronoun *I don't know if the subject is male.* To me, that makes the male pronoun less valuable and less valued. The language doesn't feel the need to be specific about men. Yes, I understand that I'm probably the only person who sees it that way, but there you go. The reason the teacher gave was probably correct, and I can see other people thinking that way, but I can't do it myself. To avoid all this trouble you'll notice I use "they" as singular just about everywhere in this book, even though that mixing of singular and plural bugs me. My daughter uses "they" until she knows a person fairly well because "he" and "she" are very specific to her.

●

We're pretty weird about death. Even elephants don't mourn their dead as much as we do, and when it comes to our own mortality we're even stranger. We all die, we all know we all die, and yet, somehow, we never seem to be ready for it. Anything else I say about it will be pretty much guaranteed to annoy just about everyone, so I'll just share this:

My dad was living on subsidized time. He'd been on disability for about 5 years. Back then, his doctors gave him 18 months to live unless he took new meds for his emphysema, arthritis, lupus, and a fourth one to keep the drug interactions of the others from killing him on the spot. One New Year's Day I was taking a shower before going to visit him in the hospital and I felt a *snap* in my chest like a taut, stretched line suddenly breaking. I'm grateful it didn't snap back and hit me in the face! What it did do is tell me that a bond had been broken. When we got to the hospital they told me what I already knew. Dad was gone.

So I was fortunate that time. I had warning. I had time to say what I needed to, to mend some fences that needed mending. To get back in

66

touch with a side of a man I'd almost forgotten. Many of my friends didn't get enough time to do that, so I'll give you the advice they gave me: *take it now.* You'll mourn less later, and regrets for people who are no longer, can never be set right.

•

Things happen, good and bad. The dance of Chaos ensures that these things will be scattered around. Good things will happen to everyone and bad things will happen to everyone. This means that bad things will happen to good people, including you. Be ready for it, and deal with it.

•

Our universe is a very strange place when you look closely. The closer you look the stranger and less intuitive it gets. Quantum Mechanics is so bizarre that "strangeness" is an actual technical term in the field. So many of the things we take for granted are dependent on QM to work at all. Without QM there would be no solar cells or nuclear reactions. The sun wouldn't work. There would be no transistors, and without them... nothing digital at all: no computers, electronic ignition, smart phones, MP3 anything, CDs, DVDs, HDTV, the list goes on and on and on.

But QM breaks down completely if Quantum Entanglement isn't possible. With QE you can entangle two or more particles so that even when they're far apart they change state together. Wiggle one and the other wiggles the same way without any detectable signal between them. The ultimate secure radio is being worked on using this. Einstein hated this "spooky action at a distance," but the whole universe falls apart if it doesn't work! Why?

The only reason I can come up with is that moving information around the universe is part of its basic function. As I understand it, if the energy density in a region of space exceeds a certain threshold while the mass density remains below another threshold, then a new Universe will inflate. The rate and scope of inflation are relative to that energy density, and during inflation the laws of physics are mutable. Sounds like a great hyperdrive to me!

67

THE EMPIRE HAS NO CLOTHES!

Suppose, now, that the MIT fratboy (or girl or squid or whatever) inventing this drive has an accident. Or someone operating one of these realizes it's going wrong. Either way, the drive gets out of control. Too much energy gets released. Said person's last thought, the one that defines the laws of physics for the new universe: "I've got to survive this!" That makes Quantum Entanglement the fundamental building block to make everything else out of.

God is a bus driver from another universe. It's no more outlandish than anything else I've heard.

"Go Greyhound, and leave... well... everything to us."

My point is that there are a lot of ideas about God, and while they seem to make sense to us at some level, because it's us limited humans trying to define it, they're all going to be wrong in some way. At some level, we may all be right, but the more we try to get at the details the more likely we are to really blow it. If God really is out there, it's unlike anything any of us can fully imagine. Let's stop fighting over it.

●

All people deserve respect until proven otherwise. Starting off with respect for others will pay back in kind. "Respect has to be earned" is a recipe for mutual, unearned disrespect. If you go in expecting others to try to earn your respect before you'll treat them with any, all you're going to get is immediate and well-earned disrespect from others for being arrogant.

●

Never attribute to malice what can be resigned to stupidity. Most people aren't evil, just careless. If most people were evil we'd all be dead by now.

●

"I have never met a man so ignorant that I couldn't learn something from him." - Galileo Galilei

●

68

Little Things

Don't confuse ignorance with stupidity. I know many very smart people of little education and many well-educated fools. To be fair, I also know a lot of very well-educated, smart people, too.

•

Nobility spent on behalf of bad people is wasted. While everyone is encouraged to be noble, no one is required to be[18]. If your nobility is being wasted, stop giving it because it has become a negative-sum game. I know several noblemen who spend a great deal of their effort and fortune supporting relatives in times of "need." In turn, the relatives then expect the support and support themselves even less. One of these noble friends fell on hard times and lost his home, and those he supported now resent him! The beneficiaries of nobility have an obligation to use it to improve their condition in such a way that they no longer need the charity. An old saying says, "lend money to a bad debtor and he will hate you for it."

•

"Anyone who keeps the ability to see beauty never grows old" - Franz Kafka.

Whether it's poetry, music, art, nature, the human form, or any other place, appreciating beauty creates something for free: it gives comfort and happiness. It's good for the soul, the mind, and the body. Anyone who has, cares for, and displays beauty should be grateful when that beauty is appreciated. They are doing good for people and can take great joy in that. One who works hard at beauty in any form and is then offended when people appreciate it is being hypocritical - and stupid. People who create beauty for the enjoyment of others create joy.

•

Never fail to create joy. If ever there was a positive-sum game, joy is it. "Sadness shared is sadness divided, but joy shared is joy multiplied." If you can make someone happy at no cost to anyone else, you've done a

---

18 Certain social contracts, as with governments taxing the people to perform services that benefit everyone, are exceptions. I'm talking here about individuals dealing with others.

wonderful thing.[19] Happiness promotes good health, both physical and mental. Joy is a real fighter of entropy and it's completely free! Creating joy may just be one of the highest purposes life can achieve. Just don't do it by creating misery for others.

•

If you're offended by something, find out why. Talk to the person or persons offending you, offer your point of view and be open to theirs. An educated mind can entertain an idea without accepting it. We've lost that. After an idea has been entertained, it can be judged on its own merits. We're all wired to fear what we don't understand. What you don't understand (a lion, a bear, or a nest of killer bees) might kill you, after all. We're also wired to be curious so we can understand which things really are dangerous. You don't have to agree with an idea to understand it, so don't let understanding frighten you. You might learn that something you fear is really a good thing, after all.

This goes double if you've offended someone else. Find out how and work out a way to fix it.

•

Never be ashamed of the way you were born. It wasn't your choice, and there's absolutely nothing you can do about it. Color, ethnicity, nationality, and physical ability have absolutely no bearing on your moral character or application of intellect, wisdom, skill, or other genuine value to society. Fancy clothes and cosmetic surgery don't, either. You are what you make of yourself and your appearance will never change that.

•

Never hate or be ashamed of the way someone else was born. Could just as easily been you.

•

Good people make mistakes, too. Goodness and nobility don't imply perfection. You aren't negligent if you've made a good faith effort to

_____

19 If someone else having joy troubles you, then you have problems.

foresee consequences and has missed some. No one can foresee everything, and it's the duty of everyone at all times to be alert. Because even good people make mistakes, good people will occasionally do bad things. If they keep good company, then they will do bad things to good people. That's life.

•

If you quite fairly get what you asked for, don't complain. Even if it's not what you wanted. This goes double for people who force negative-sum games on others and end up losing. A burglar has no right to sue the homeowner for injuries sustained while bungling the burgling!

•

Blaming someone else because you were stupid, careless, or negligent is wrong. Ignorance and stupidity are not the same things: ignorance is the temporary lack of some piece of knowledge; stupidity is the lack of mental reasoning ability or the unwillingness to apply it. Don't be stupid.

•

"Trying to save someone from their own stupidity is like trying to teach a pig how to dance: it wastes your time, and annoys the pig." - Robert A. Heinlein

•

Forgive failure, punish intent. We all fail at some time or another. It's a rare occasion when it's appropriate to punish failure, and that's usually when the one who failed began lying about it to cover it up. The cover-up starts a negative-sum game that's bad for all. Negligence (not *gross negligence*) normally deserves lighter punishment than intent.

•

Of course people can echo locate like bats. On a late-night, moonless harassment patrol with the Marines I realized I was tripping over a bunch of stuff. By Marine Corps standards, anyway. I hadn't done that last time... what was different? "Ear plugs." I took them out and immediately I stopped my little stumbles. I realized right then that the only way that could be is if I was hearing the slight echoes of my

71

footfalls off of branches and other obstacles. I never wore protection (hearing protection!) while creeping through the woods again.

•

No idea is so dangerous that it must be suppressed. No matter how vehemently you disagree with it, and no matter how contrary it may be to established historical fact, all ideas should be allowed their day in the sun. A society that can't survive rational discourse on ideas *should not survive.* If an idea is so terrible, then *it* won't survive. Sure, there are *facts* that should be kept secret, like how to make certain terrible weapons, but *ideas* are the lifeblood of society and the true form of our diversity. They are our strength. The far left tries to control speech while the far right tries to ban and destroy books. When you reach those extremes, it gets hard to tell one set of extremists from another: they're all the same in their desire to control the minds of others. Controlling others' minds prevents new ideas, and that's a very negative-sum game.

That said, Justice Oliver Wendell Holmes was right when he said, "The most stringent protection of free speech would not protect a man in falsely shouting fire in a theatre and causing a panic." While not false, I've had one or two ideas that, if I said them publicly, would probably provoke some violent, irrational people to horrible, unjustifiable acts for wholly illegitimate reasons. No, I won't tell you what they are. The very best thing about this book is that I've taken them out.

No idea is so dangerous that it must be suppressed, but be careful what you *do* with those ideas. Don't act on every idea you have, and don't believe everything you think.

I'm not the only one to notice things. Some of these people's observations have informed my own. They said good stuff. Some are no longer popular, but their observations remain true.

●

"Censorship reflects society's lack of confidence in itself."

  - Potter Stewart

●

"The greatest dangers to liberty lurk in insidious encroachment by men of zeal, well-meaning but without understanding."

  - Supreme Court Justice Louis D. Brandeis

●

"Either you think -- or else others have to think for you and take power from you, pervert and discipline your natural tastes, civilize and sterilize you."

  - F. Scott Fitzgerald

●

"Excellence does not require perfection."

  - Henry James

●

"If you always tell the truth, you don't have to remember anything."

  - Mark Twain

●

"The three types of lies are, in order: Lies; Damned Lies; and, Statistics."

  - Mark Twain.

Any time you see a statistic, remember the one rule that many forget: it has to make sense. Sure, you may find a numerical correlation between the most popular color of house paint in Paris and the number of fish in the Yangtze River, but it's safe to say that that's nothing more than a

THE EMPIRE HAS NO CLOTHES!

coincidence. Can you think of a mechanism that would tie those together? Be open to explanation and be willing to understand, but be cautious, too. As statisticians warn: "correlation does not imply causation." Most conspiracy theories are based on the assumption that it does.

●

"A doubtful friend is worse than a certain enemy. Let a man be one thing or the other, and we then know how to meet him."

   - Aesop

●

"I have some good friends who occasionally can be unpleasant. But none of my good friends are ever dishonest."

   - Eolake Stobblehouse

●

"The first duty of a citizen is not to vote, but to be informed."

   - Thomas Jefferson

●

"I don't know the key to success, but the key to failure is trying to please everybody."

   -Bill Cosby

●

"To laugh often and much; to win the respect of intelligent people and the affection of children; to earn the appreciation of honest critics and endure the betrayal of false friends; to appreciate beauty; to find the best in others; to leave the world a bit better, whether by a healthy child, a garden patch or a redeemed social condition; to know even one life has breathed easier because you have lived. This is to have succeeded."

   - Emerson

74

I've managed to achieve all of Emerson's measures of success. I've had the good fortune to save at least one life, had a direct hand in saving three others, and turn some around for the better. And my daughter, well, I think she's amazing. She understands at sixteen what it's taken me a lifetime to get. If the world is a better place because of her, and I have no doubt that it will be, then perhaps I will have succeeded again, and I will be in her debt beyond all measure.

●

And finally, from Socrates himself:

The man who sees others as his inferiors has none.

Boomers

I'm a baby boomer, one of the last. I was born just over a year before the assassination of JFK brought the boom to an end as abruptly as the end of World War II had started it. Baby boomers, it seems to me, are the most self-absorbed generation in history. The "me" generation, and "My Way" was written in part as its anthem. Sure, there are lots of great exceptions, but as a group we're more bizarre than any other generation I know of.

When World War II ended, the GI Generation justifiably became involved in the moment. Most of my peers, including my wife, had parents who served in that war. My eldest uncle didn't return, having been shot down in the pre-dawn night after his 21st birthday while flying home from a bombing mission. When those who did return, returned, they were tired of war and had served enough public duty to last a century. They took a laissez-faire attitude socially and economically. Leave everyone to their own thing, and everything will be great. After the second world war they wanted it, even needed it, so they believed it. And it was that way mostly, so the GG men went off and built stuff. Lots of stuff. Bombers and cargo vessels and ICBMs and refineries and computers and moon ships and ski resorts. Everything but families. They weren't all that way, but a lot were. Lots of the new jobs were engineering jobs in the new, permanent military-industrial complex, and they weren't the same as their fathers' jobs. No bringing the kids to the shop or the smithy to teach them the family trade. These jobs took concentration, collaboration, and sometimes a security clearance. Their children were ruled over and expected to take care of themselves, and they left their homes early because they wanted to live somewhere better. Nothing wrong with that, but a lot of Boomers walked out with the understanding that the only life anyone cared about was his own and they took it to heart. Enough to really ruin things. As a group they responded in two big ways, both of them bad. Either they railed against the Empire in every conceivable form, calling for small-scale socialism, agrarianism, free love, and no police or military; or they became the Empire, seeking to place themselves above the law, cheating regulations, bribing inspectors, plundering from it what they could and caring nothing for others. Many of them lost sight of consequence for anyone but themselves. Why that happened so much more than it usually does had much more to do with big business and chemistry than it had to do with families,[20] and it happened regardless of parents, culture, nationality, or genetics. And it had happened before.

Boomers and Romans

At the end of the war, there was an economic boom and between the crates of 4 for $25 surplus jeeps and lots of new cars being bought, we hit the road in record numbers. "Road trip!" was the rallying cry of the late 1940s and 1950s. Everyone was working (well, everyone white and male and a few women who kept their wartime jobs into the new era) and their families were prosperous. Leisure time and disposable income were everywhere. Everything was great for them, except they were poisoning themselves doing it. I think that part isn't so great – in fact, it sucks more than just a little. We did it with exhaust fumes full of tetraethyl lead (TEL), fully knowing lead's illustrious history. It was there because it was a cheap way to boost the octane rating of fuel, and it was known to be toxic before it was even tried.

"Let's go out for a picnic."

"Sounds great! I'll bring the powdered donuts and rat poison."

As lead levels in the atmosphere rose, they rose in our blood, too.

---

20 Mother Jones, Jan/Feb 2013. "Lead: America's Real Criminal Element"

THE EMPIRE HAS NO CLOTHES!

Lead, even in small amounts, poisons the brain. It's especially hard on developing brains. The babies got hit hard and we wouldn't know it for decades.

This is your brain.

This is your brain on lead.

Any questions?[21]

Human brains that develop under exposure to lead are broken in ways that make for poor decision-making ability. Even if you're

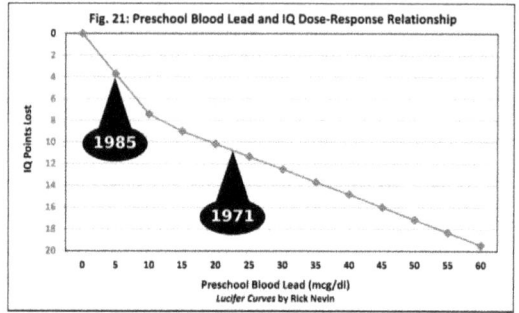

Fig. 21: Preschool Blood Lead and IQ Dose-Response Relationship

a Boomer or Gen-Xer and you make great decisions, I'll bet they would have been even better without lead. Just look at what happens when babies exposed to lead grow up! This is why high school IQ scores have been on the rise lately.

Expose every baby and child to lead and violent crime jumps 23 years later – not because lead makes everyone into raving lunatics, but because it impairs rational decision-making and increases your chances of acting stupidly. Ban leaded gasoline, and violence goes

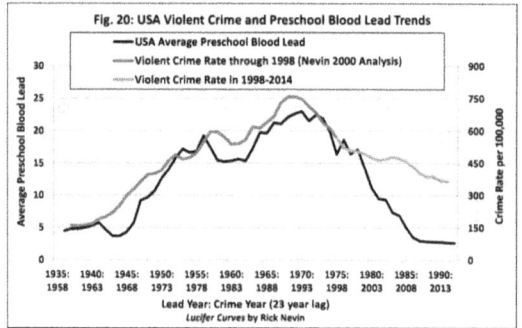

Fig. 20: USA Violent Crime and Preschool Blood Lead Trends

back down 23 years later. People make better decisions.

Teen pregnancy rates did much the same, though given the looser match there do appear to be other things involved: social inertia and pressure, the Empire.

---

21 "1971" and "1985" annotations by the author. Charts from Rick Nevin's book, "Lucifer Curves" and RickNevin.com. The other data there just show how important lead remediation around the world really is. And how bad things will be in Flint in 15 years.

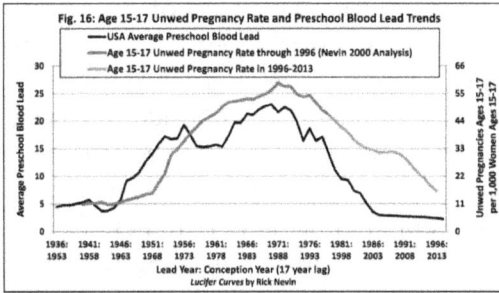

Fig. 16: Age 15-17 Unwed Pregnancy Rate and Preschool Blood Lead Trends

It was big business greed that nearly wiped us all out, and big government in the form of the EPA that enforced the ban that saved us. Next time someone tries to tell you that government is always the problem, well, now you know better. "An exception to the rule," you say? Maybe, but even if so it's the kind of exception we can't ever afford to miss.

The Roman Empire loved its lead. The Latin word for lead, "plumbite," is the root word for plumbing. They used it in water pipes, wine goblets, even make-up. They wore it and drank it – we breathed it. In a few generations the Roman emperors fell from the likes of Julius and Augustus to Caligula. Need I say more?

Boomers and Government

William Jefferson Clinton was the first American president born after World War 2. The first Baby Boomer president. He was opposed by a congress also largely born after WWII. The boomers had taken over. The idealists on both sides have been at counterproductive, uncompromising loggerheads ever since. It's a mess. Obviously, these early Boomers had less lead in their environment, but how often were they, as small children, allowed up close to it to (help) pump the gas? I know I used to bite sinkers closed sometimes when dad and I went fishing even though he told me not to. How common was that?

The Boomers lived through three decades of increasing crime. They grew up with it and they thought it was normal. Their parents thought it was a failing of culture. They both blamed it on the social upheaval of the 1960s, "weak" sentencing, not enough police, the breakdown of society, whatever. They set about turning America's police into military organizations.

THE EMPIRE HAS NO CLOTHES!

Around the time the Boomers took power, the effects of falling lead exposure started to show. 1970 was the worst year for lead in the air, and 1993 was the worst year for crime. I guess it takes a while. I guess infants don't commit many violent crimes, unless you consider throwing up to be a violent crime. The Boomers on both sides of the aisle took credit for the two decades of increasing safety that followed, pointing to "broken window" policing in New York and many other things. Maybe those helped, but when you can follow the lead by following the crime everywhere on Earth, you've got to admit that lead is the major part of it.

America's next generation had a hard time finding its way between the ever more extreme left and right. Not that there wasn't a lot of room in the middle, it's just that they were forced to choose one side or the other (don't do it!), when neither extreme really appealed to most of them. It took them time to find their way, and impatient Boomers derided them as "Generation X." As if being unable to be pigeonholed were somehow a bad thing. They, too, were a leaded generation, possibly the most leaded generation since the fall of Rome.

In 1970, US lead output into the atmosphere began to drop, and by the end of 1985 it was essentially gone. Crime is back down to the levels of more than 50 years ago. Anyone who tells you different, wants something from you. Probably money or power. Or both. It was the scientists and environmentalists, not the legislatures or police, who saved us from that crime wave.

The New Middle East Problem

Most of the Middle East, including Yemen, Syria, and Iran, continued using TEL in their gasoline until just a few years ago. North Korea may still be using it – we don't know for sure. All we have to do is wait out the next 20 years! Chill! We don't have to fight another war; all we have to do is wait. If we stay out of their business we'll stay out of their sights and *for the most part* they'll fight among themselves until arrest, attrition, and a new unleaded generation remove them from the equation. Let them make their own bad decisions, and let each country deal with its own problems as much as possible. The world does still look to America for leadership, not because we're perfect but because we're good and capable. Let's do it like we did under the Marshall Plan. Help when it is asked for – generously – and lead by example.

Leaded gasoline use declined dramatically during the US phase-out that started in 1975 and ended in its being banned in 1996. Most of Europe banned it in 2000 (new cars using it were banned from sale in 1992). In late 2011, leaded gasoline was still available at the pump Algeria, Iraq, Yemen, Myanmar, North Korea, and Afghanistan. No, that list doesn't sound familiar at all, does it? Only Algeria, Iraq, and Yemen still use it.

Sure, there'll be problems that do affect us,[22] but when aren't there? It's getting better and the last trouble spots will only be this elevated kind of trouble for about 20 more years. We'll need to fight a lot of holding actions as we ride the crest of this wave, but it will subside. Assuming we align our policy with that understanding, and work toward improving agency and economics for the rest of the world like we did after WWII, we'll see a drastic drop in recruitment and action by bad people in these leaded regions.

What we are is part predisposition and part experience. In some people those predispositions are too strong to overcome with any amount of training – especially when amplified by lead exposure. Thankfully, most of us can learn to overcome them. Thanks to the wild variation of human biochemistry we'll never be rid of these people completely,[23] but please let's not go to war over a problem that's already mostly solved. Be patient!

One of the biggest things the west can do to reduce tensions and reassure the middle east that we don't have a dark political objective there

22 Lead isn't our only problem, after all! We have lots of issues.
23 This is the best argument I know for *encouraging* abortion in cases of rape: the biochemistry that drove the violence are present in the "father" and likely to be passed on to the new generation. Forcing rape victims to carry to term compounds the crime in more ways than just denying the victim the chance to move on. The sins of the fathers are indeed visited upon the children and the grandchildren.

is to not have even the appearance of one. We can achieve that while realizing new 21st century jobs and cutting imports. All of these positive goals are tied to the same thing and have the same solution: divesting ourselves of the biggest national security problem America and Europe face. The same interest that ties our hands also compels us to be involved more than we should. That thing is oil. So much of our foreign policy is centered around a stable supply of oil that we can't take the long view or risk any change in the supply chain. We support a lot of things we shouldn't because we can't afford for the owner of my fuel to be my enemy.

Renewable energy sources are more reliable than the existing energy Empire wants you to know. Microgeneration and utility-scale generation in the form of solar, wind, geothermal, and hydro don't have to replace everything. They just have to replace imports for now, and when that happens America's economy is stronger and its security is greater. Energy independence is inherently patriotic. The same goes for Europe and other energy importers. Of course, that means that oil isn't as big an economic force in the middle east, but then those nations can – and eventually must, anyway – do as Dubai has done. Dubai long ago realized that its future wasn't measured in years, but in barrels, and set out to reinvent itself. It's become the upscale tourist destination for the very wealthy. *Seven*-star hotel, anyone? The other OPEC nations have a great deal of money and the energy supplies to reinvent themselves, as well, and Dubai just built a solar power farm for less than six cents a kilowatt-hour. Cheaper than gas. Like Dubai, and coal miners, and lots of other 19th and 20th century industries and lifestyles, change is coming. It's better if we all decide on these changes in advance and help each other through them when we can, rather than wait and have to fight over dwindling resources later. And it'll be great if when the age of oil power is over we still have a lot of it left. Making plastics and other things is a much better use for it that just burning it up.

The Millennials

Millennials are America's first generation since the late 1920s born without lead on their brains.[24]   The Greatest Generation were the last before them. From 1958 to 1978, lead levels were crazy high. These are the parents of the Millennials.   Their guidance may have been problematic, but the Millennials seem to be working it out. Born starting in 1985, the year lead levels in the air dropped below 1937 levels, many of them are clever, motivated, adept people who start novel companies and do things more differently and pay people better than Boomers think is rational.   They do a lot of experiments in their social and business lives. Even if some of them are famously entitled or oversensitive (due mostly to their leadite helicopter parents) as a group they're less afraid than their parents or grandparents, and with good reason.   "You of tender years can't know the fears that your elders grew by."   And to a large extent they'll never need to. They share cars, bikes, apartments, and even plates at dinner out. Part of that is economic necessity, but it's also a sea change in society. They're getting out there and figuring it out.

In Africa there's a word for this: Ubuntu. Nelson Mandela described it this way: "A traveller through a country would stop at a village and he didn't have to ask for food or for water. Once he stops, the people give him food and attend him. That is one aspect of Ubuntu, but it will have various aspects. Ubuntu does not mean that people should not enrich themselves. The question therefore is: Are you going to do so in order to enable the community around you to be able to improve?"

Archbishop Desmond Tutu defined Ubuntu in his 1999 book, *No Future Without Forgiveness*: "A person with Ubuntu is open and available to others, affirming of others, does not feel threatened that others are able and good, based from a proper self-assurance that comes from knowing that he or she belongs in a greater whole and is diminished when others are humiliated or diminished, when others are tortured or oppressed."

If there's a reason why humans are so very social, then it's to achieve Ubuntu, to understand that we are never completely alone but that some aspect of our society is always with us.   All the interdependence that

---

24 Okay, not completely, but still wow! There's still TEL in the soil, but there's almost none in the air, and no lead in new house paint or toys. Lead poisoning has been almost unheard-of in the United States for over 30 years. Let's make it better still.

makes our society complex, also gives us greater agency as individuals. That is the root of Ubuntu. The flower of it is what Nelson Mandela and Archbishop Desmond Tutu spoke about. Taken together, you could summarize it as "I am because we are." Without the good the Empire does for us, then what we are is very different and distinctly less; but we've seen already that while the Empire's clothes make things simpler they don't always make things better. Around here Ubuntu is buried under a landslide of Adam Smith rugged individualism and every-man-for-himself. Smith was wrong; Nash was right.

Millennials are changing everything and I see a real sense of Ubuntu in a lot of them. I think they see their place in the Empire and the world more clearly than any first-world generation since the dawn of the Industrial Revolution, and much more clearly than I see my own. I can't help but believe that when the first clear-thinking American generation in nearly a century finally finds its way into power, the entire world will be the better for it. Personally, I can't wait to see what minds immeasurably cleaner than mine[25] can come up with. The first generation born to the first lead-free generation will be even better. It's taken the Millennials a while to figure out the world and given their environment I'm not surprised, but figure it out they do, and they do it largely on their own. Between the lead and the changes in technology, it's a fresh outlook that probably few Boomers or Gen-Xers or even GGs will ever comprehend.

Perhaps more than any generation since the Greatest, Millennials don't change things so they can make money. They make money by changing things.[26] They're dissatisfied with the quality of life and set out to improve it for its own sake. That they can make a living doing so only makes it more meaningful. In that I see a lot of myself in them. In a job interview I was asked, "what technology excites you." My answer was an instant, "whatever technology solves the problem."

---

25 Apologies to H. G. Wells!

26 Don't get me wrong, they're more aware of "money is power" than anyone since the 19th century robber barons. That may be a problem that counterbalances their Ubuntu, or maybe that balance is what we need. Vote for individuals, vote carefully. And can we elect some doctors and engineers and stuff instead of just lawyers? Step up, people! Run!

When asked in that same interview, "what do you want to do," I replied, "make a difference." The interviewer responded with a bored, almost annoyed, "yes, but what are you passionate about." I replied, "if I haven't made a difference in my life, then my life is wasted. I want to know what your problems are and how I can best contribute to solving them." I didn't get the job. A lot of my peers and seniors just don't seem to be able to understand that *making a difference is all I want to do.* While making a living is something I need to do, I have too much to do in this life to waste it making a living.[27] More Millennials seem to get this than any other generation.

The baby boom ran about 20 years, but the Boomers aren't giving up control. No one except George Washington ever has. Want to "take back America" or just "make it great again?" Want to save the world? Take it out of the hands of the Boomers. It's time for the <u>late</u> Generation Xers and Millennials to step up! Lots of you are old enough. Your time is upon you. With billionaire and near-billionaire entrepreneurs from Facebook, Instagram, Dropbox, Spotify, Wordpress, and others, there's certainly enough business cred to make it happen. You have military and civil service positions. You can do this.

Look at those curves a few pages back. In terms of Congress, can we please skip just about everyone born from about 1948 to 1985? Not just America but Greece, Spain, Britain, Russia, the Middle East, and the whole world? Russia, Syria, and North Korea in aprticular are going to come along slower, because they gave up lead later, but the principle is the same: we need to get the power out of the hands of the leadites. It's going to take time and loads of diplomatic and political effort, and now isn't the time for pointless saber rattling.

Nearly a quarter century ago we hit the lead-induced peak of crime in the United States and much of the world, and it's been getting better ever since. Now the lead-induced peak of stupid is setting its sights on our

---

27 To that end, I should probably have paid more attention to money early in my career, but everyone else was all "money, money, money," and it was revolting. Now they're seeking their first truly meaningful jobs and I've had a life full of them; they're flush with money and I'm finally seeking it.

government and big business. Violent criminals average closer to 23 while US House and Senate members average closer to 60, so naturally the increase in stupid government would lag almost 40 years behind. If things continue as they are, the Stupid peak should be around 2030 and persist at or above current levels until around 2040-2045. If we can get through this troubled period, and that's by no means certain at this point, then we can not only get through anything but we can make everything better for our posterity. Fortunately, there are elections in government so we can skip it if we have the will. This is a call to action! Millennials have to not only get out and vote, but they have to run! It's about communities: rural, urban, and international. If any generation understands community better than the Millennials, I don't know who it is; and community is an excellent focus around which to build foreign and domestic policy.

Term limits might help, but I can't see members of Congress ever voting against their own personal power. Maybe clearer minds can see beyond their own self-interest again. "Country above party" needs to come back to the U.S., like it is with the French center-right. It would be wonderful to see our public servants actually serve us once more. It can and will happen.

Love

The Empire tells us a lot about love, and most of it's wrong. The Empire treats love as if it were some kind of limited resource. It isn't. Our awareness of it may be, but our love itself is unlimited.

You'll Love Like That Again

No, you won't. Not ever. Every time you love, it's different. Not necessarily greater, or lesser, just different. Like pie, you can have apple, cheery, blackberry, and key lime; and, at moments, choose to spend your time with one of them over the others, but they're all good. All are real and true, and each is unique. So it is with love. With one exception all the people I've ever loved, I still do. They're all different, all wonderful, and I wouldn't trade any of them for... well... a bunch of cool stuff.

With All My Heart

"I love you with all my heart." Got kids? "I'm sorry, kiddo – I love your mother with all my heart so you're out of luck." It just doesn't work that way. I love my wife bunches. I love my daughter to pieces. The love I feel for one in no way diminishes the other. The love I have for my friends, old loves, relations, and others diminishes nothing.

87

THE EMPIRE HAS NO CLOTHES!

There's Someone for Everyone

Wrong again. Not all of us even *want* the kind of relationship that implies, and not all who do ever find it. True, the amazing diversity of people pretty much ensures that everyone will eventually meet someone who's really good for them – and that they are really good for. It also ensures that a few of us will be outside the envelope of our culture, so no one else in that culture will fill the need. Some of them will be able to use the Internet (information is the key to agency) to find someone far away that they would never otherwise meet. Still others will live alone, some by choice, some in quiet confidence, and some in desperation.

Your Other Half

You're not half a person and no one is going to "complete" you. No one but you is going to make you a complete person. You need to have your own goals, your own interests, your own life. *You need to complete yourself.* Sure, you may *feel* vaguely incomplete, but that's an illusion. We have basic drives as highly social beings that reproduce sexually. The expression of those drives changes once we've gone from unfocused desire to actually doing someone about them. It's a fulfillment of basic drives, and an application of our agency to that end. It's a drive finding expression and focus, not ourselves completed.

Don't get me wrong. My wife fills in for my weaknesses and I fill in for hers. We complement, support, and reinforce each other. We're a lot stronger together than apart; but we were both complete people with our own interests, hobbies, skills, and talents before we met. She doesn't complete me and I don't complete her. We make each others' *lives* more complete, not each other.

Real Love is Jealous

Jealousy has no place in the life or love of a sane person. I know many people who love, and make love with, many people. There's no jealousy there, and if on some rare occasion there is, they all talk about it and work out why it's there so something can be done about it.

I know what I'm talking about here. I spent much time and effort banishing jealousy from my life because I realized that mine was so powerful that it would leave me dead. It doesn't make you stronger, it just makes you *feel* strong. It's a fighting response to something that should never be a fighting situation. Jealousy is the fast road to the Dark Side. We don't need it to protect those we love. We just need love.

I use the word jealousy carefully. While jealousy's root is insecurity, it's a lot more than that. To me jealousy is a lot like envy, but different. Insecurity is not knowing how strong or stable your possession of something, or relationship to something or someone, is. Envy is wanting something someone else has. Jealousy is an intense fear of losing something you already have (or feel you have or are about to have) to someone else, often in a context where there's no sense of agency. If you feel powerless to prevent a loss, you become desperate. Desperate people, like cornered animals, are dangerous. Jealousy is one of the main causes of violence. We don't need it and we can live without it, but doing so takes work. Trust me, it's worth it.

One True Love

So every other time I've thought I've loved, I haven't? I don't buy that. Not "for a dollar" or for anything. I've got news for you: I've loved many, and with one exception who went out of her way to earn her exception, I still love all of them. That I love my wife differently doesn't mean the others aren't true. All love is true. Just be sure that it's love, and not just lust or a desire to control, that you're feeling.

Ironically, with the Empire telling us so much about love that's false, a series of movies about a galactic empire tell us a some things about love that are true. Love can make you strong, or it can make you weak. Love, desire, and the fear of loss made Anakin weak. His overriding and unachievable desire, to live openly with his love, made his power not be enough. He wanted more and pursued it greedily in the hope that it would give him the agency he longed for. The Emperor was able to play on that desperation to twist Anakin's beliefs to justify actions he was fooled into taking. His true friends failed him in that regard. The dogma of a long-established order could find no quarter for his love, and in the end he parted ways with that order.

Luke, on the other hand, was strengthened by his love. The rage that drove him to defeat his father, rage that the Emperor thought was hate, was love. He found within himself and his circumstances the power to protect those he loved, and used that power to its fullest. The Emperor never turned him, and in the end he gave Darth Vader the power to do for him what Darth had repeatedly failed to do for others before. Your love can save others as surely as it can save you.

Marriage is Changing

For millennia in many cultures marriage has been a political and economic institution, arranged by the parents without consulting the ones most affected by it. In other words, imposed upon them: unethical. Only recently do people marry for love, and they leave their marriages if the love is gone. Love overcame marriage, as one writer put it. It's taken a long time to expose this emperor's nudity so we could see each other's! Life is fun again!

Marriage is also changing in ways that more resemble our free-loving, hunter-gatherer tribal past. Group marriages, while not yet legally recognized, are becoming more common and socially accepted – albeit very slowly. If having two parents is "stable," then having six or eight or ten must be more stable – and exponentially more complicated! At least then if one has to leave it's less traumatic because the child hasn't lost half their parents, nor the teamwork of multiple parents. If one loses a job it's also less traumatic. That one could even go back to college for a new degree without worrying that the family will starve. In an economy changing as rapidly as ours is (and that's speeding up), going back to school is going to become a necessity – maybe even twice in each person's working life. Group marriages can give people the economic stability to go back to school and start over in new careers.

Sex

"Life in Lubbock, Texas taught me ... that sex is the most awful, filthy thing on earth, and you should save it for someone you love."

- Butch Hancock

The Empire tells us a lot about sex, and what it tells each of us depends a lot on who and where we are. It tells us that humans naturally and exclusively pair-bond for life. That joy shared is joy multiplied – except for sex. That it's different from every other aspect of life and has to be kept separate, hidden, not discussed in detail. That it's only good for procreation and advertising. That there's something morally repugnant about it, and there's something wrong with you if you enjoy it. That a woman who says "yes" is loose (therefore bad) and one who says "no" is frigid (therefore bad); but that a man who does either is being a real man.

The Empire tries to put more rules and restrictions on it than are good for us, and we suffer for it. I'm not just talking about monotony of sex, but about the kind of pain that the implicit or explicit expectation of monogamy creates when that expectation isn't met.

But it's So Much Fun!

So if sex is so much fun, and we all know it is, why are human beings naturally monogamous? The truth is that we aren't and we never have been. It's a lie we tell ourselves to preserve the Empire as we know it.

91

THE EMPIRE HAS NO CLOTHES!

Think about it this way. In most countries, there are laws against sex outside of marriage. Why do they exist at all? If monogamous pair bonding were our natural state of affairs (!), we wouldn't need laws about it. Yet we have such laws. Some involve the death penalty, and still people break them. You don't need laws or threat of death to force people to do what comes naturally; you need laws to make people to obey rules that are contrary to their nature. Monogamy and marriage are artificial constructs. They work well for some of us, but as divorce statistics show, they aren't working for an awful lot of us.

The Empire expects us to expect our partners to be monogamous. Great – one more thing to be afraid of! That expectation and the underlying fear that any violation of it must be devastating and the end of the relationship creates a lot of jealousy in the world, and jealousy is the source of a lot of violence. If more of us understood that people sometimes wander, that they need a little variety, and that even so they're still coming home to the family, I think we'd have a lot less domestic violence and a lot more adventures with our partners. And a lot more to talk about!

"Hello, dear. Do anyone interesting today?"

We also know that in most monogamous relationships sexual attraction to the partner starts to wane after only two years, on average. The "seven year itch" isn't cynical, it's actually quite generous.

"Seven year itch?"

"Why, yes, thank you. That's very generous of you."

"It's my pleasure."

Variety is the spice of life. If the plural of mouse is mice, then the plural of spouse should be spice, and maybe that fits better than we were led to believe!

Playing Around

Infidelity isn't an exclusively human trait, and we're learning that even animals that "pair bond" and mate for life often leave the nest for a little copulatory recreation. Males and females alike. It's simple: if the purpose of life is to make more life then life that reproduces sexually will go to great lengths for sex and to ensure reproduction. It increases genetic diversity and it's perfectly natural.

That it's natural doesn't make it right or wrong; it just makes it natural. The Empire tells you it's always wrong, and it's losing that battle. So much the better. The Empire has also worked very hard to make it hard to talk about. That's not good. If any partner in a marriage engages in an unapproved sexual affair, taking an increased risk of disease, pregnancy, love, and other nasty effects, that partner then brings that increased risk home and exposes the other partner to them – without consent. In our culture (and the 15% of human cultures that have been predominantly monogamous) one must also consider jealousy, alienation of affection, breach of trust and other such matters.

These things increase the risks for the partners that don't go on the tryst, so all partners' informed consent *must* be obtained *in advance*. How might a pregnancy affect a nonparticipating partner? How about the responsibility the participants must take on and the impact on the families' ability to support themselves? All of these things and more must be carefully weighed and considered. Keeping secrets only compounds the problem.

The important thing is to talk about it. Discuss these issues *before* getting married (gay, straight, group, or whatever) and then live within the bounds agreed upon. If agreement cannot be reached, then you can't have a contract or covenant. It's that simple. My wife and I were very clear on these matters before we married, so we are very secure. I have no need to be jealous when she comments on an attractive fellow and likewise she has no need to be jealous of me. We understand looking is not the same as wanting, which is not the same as intending to act, which is not the same as trying, which is not quite the same as doing. We are free to see and enjoy human beauty, but for most of our lives together we have drawn the line at trying. Others may draw the line elsewhere, but both partners in a marriage *must know and agree* where that line is, if it exists at all, what the consequences are of crossing it, and exactly what, if any, exceptions there may be. Only then can a couple be truly secure in their relationship; and security leads to comfort, confidence, stability, and a higher sum for all.

Sex Sells

Sex sells because the Empire demands we hold it separate from all the other aspects of our lives. We can't talk about it. We can talk about everything about our children from the first trimester up to their professional lives: everything except the moment of conception.

Advertisers and media producers would like to keep it that way. You can't talk about it, but their TV shows and movies can. You can talk about it in the context of their programs, but only then. Because it's so limited and so separate, it gets our attention, and that makes it valuable to advertisers. It's an easy path to financial success.

Oddly, it's generally illegal to sell sex directly, though you can give it away for free and sell the video. No other thing we value so much has been so segregated from the rest of our lives. And when we do that, we segregate our bodies as well.

Confusion

> *"What spirit is so empty and blind, that it cannot recognize the fact that the foot is more noble than the shoe, and skin more beautiful than the garment with which it is clothed?"*

> *- Michelangelo.*

There are cultures where clothed settlers and naked indigenous people coexist without a thought about it. I live near a city that allows people to walk around nude but arrests them for flashing. It recognizes that there's a difference between dress and intent, that "nudity is not enough by itself to meet the standard of indecency." Much of the rest of the Empire needs to lose some of its clothes about our clothes:

94

"Nudity equals sexuality." Wrong. Ever take a hot shower after a hard day of physical work? The sore muscles, the heat, the steam, the water pounding on your back. Very sensual, but relaxing and not sexual at all. Sexuality is about intent, not about inches of skin covered.

"Female nudity is beautiful, but male nudity is ugly and threatening." Again, the sooner we stop assuming that nudity *must* have sexual intent, the better. Stop assuming the correlation and start allowing people to *be* as their creator made them, and the Empire will gradually stop being so afraid.

"Nudity is disgusting." We teach our children this from a very young age, before they are even able to separate identity, personality, and physicality. Before they can regard their identity separately, before body and self are separate concepts, we teach them to be ashamed, and many learn to be ashamed of themselves. Some never recover from it.

Nudity is just the ultimate in casual wear. I'm not covering up my makers' artwork with designs that elevate my "artwork" above it. I'm not hiding behind advertising or social trendiness. Clothes say a lot about where we fit into the Empire. Suit and tie, work boots, surf shorts, they all tell people more about us than our unadorned bodies alone do. By going nude we announce we have nothing to say about that at the moment and intend to do exactly that. That in itself says something important. Once we get used to seeing it, we'll stop caring. It won't matter. The Empire won't be obsessed with it any more. We'll be over it, and that'll be great.

But Why?

Why are we this way? Probably because we're more like our near cousins the bonobos than we are like our better-known near cousins the chimpanzees. Bonobos are the only other primates that use facing sexual positions (think "missionary") and they do it with just about everyone for all kinds of reasons including reinforcing social bonds ("friends with benefits"), conflict resolution ("make-up sex"), and just plain fun.

It seems that we were like them up until we invented agriculture. About then, someone noticed that new grain grew in the place where it had been stacked the year before. It didn't take long to understand the importance of seeds. An experiment was done and we found that by planting grain in one place we could grow more than we could gather. The man who did this was almost certainly a woman, since in most hunter-gather societies that's how it works: men hunt and sometimes gather, and women gather, organize, and keep count of the stores.[28] The problem with that little invention was, planting took a lot more work than gathering. We traded variety for quantity, and lives of leisure for lives of toil. That toil meant we were heavily invested in the crop, and at some point someone said, "I worked my ass off for this - see it laying in the field? This land and the crop that springs from it are MINE." Private property was born. The man who first did that was, beyond reasonable doubt, a man. At some point, the men who had divided up the land realized that they wanted to make sure that their private property went to *their* children. In sexually open societies, men can't be sure of paternity, so they invented marriage and monogamy (and given the climate in the Fertile Crescent, probably clothes) to control reproduction and protect their newfound economic interests.

Women Messed it All Up!

I think that men have long blamed women for the lack of sexual freedom that men imposed upon themselves in response to economic pressures they put on themselves in response to women's discovery that you could plant grain. We went from a very few free-loving, easy-living, laid-back hunter-gatherers working maybe 16 hours a week to a great many toiling, monogamous farmers with less variety in our diet and our sex. Truly the discovery of agriculture brought great benefit in the form of predictability and great quantity along with the bane of lesser variety, harder work, and less sex. "The fruit of the tree of knowledge of good and evil," indeed! With the end of communal property came greed. With monogamy came jealousy. With great food supplies came permanent settlements, houses, geometry (to measure the land), rapidly increasing population, and everything that's followed. With private

---

28 Women here are too valuable to risk on potentially deadly hunting trips.

property, jealousy, and occasional shortages now clearly separated by owners, came war.

What These Men Really Hate

For those men who still blame women for their problems, I think it's not the discovery but men's response to the discovery that these men really resent. We could have gone half and half on the farming versus hunter-gathering. Maybe we did and ended up warring over it. We could have not worried about whose kids got the land, or traced our lineage through the women like some other cultures. We could have kept it light, but we didn't. Come on, guys, let it go. Misogyny is is so Ten Thousand B.C.. It's our own screw-up, and it's time we admitted it.

Terrorism

Becoming a Terrorist

The Empire tells us that peaceful people become violent lunatics out of "radicalization" by some outside force and we have to prevent that by keeping those ideas out, yet at the same time we're told that domestic mass shooters "just snap," and there's nothing we can do about that. In what way, exactly, are these two people different?

One leads a quiet, unassuming life of hidden desperation until one day someone comes up to him and says, "it's okay to be violent. We don't mind." The other leads a quiet, unassuming life of hidden desperation until something – internal or external – says, "it's okay to be violent. We don't mind." They both had the potential, the desire to live in a world where they have some sense of control over their lives, and suddenly breaking the most fundamental rules seems to be the only way. Then they both set off murdering people. One we call insane and the other we call a radicalized terrorist.

I call them both insane, and they were both insane long before anyone noticed. That said, both are driven by the lack of agency they feel in their own lives and their desire to have some sense of power. Terrorists become terrorists for social or political reasons, and if they act out in the name of a religion it's because they've found a few words in it somewhere, or just a few people even, who will validate their pre-existing fight-or-flight desire to do violence. If they feel like everyone's walking all over them like a herd of club-footed caterpillars and they can't do anything about it then they're probably going to start killing caterpillars (club-footed or not) the first chance they get! Letting the caterpillars become butterflies is just not going to be acceptable in their minds. They're wrong, completely nuts in fact, but when has that ever stopped anyone?

Terrorist groups probably attract all four kinds of "hate" criminals: the thrill seekers, who don't care about anyone and don't think anyone else does, either; the "defenders" who perceive the presence of other ideas or groups as a threat; the retaliators who only want revenge and take it on innocent members of the race/religion/country they perceive as being the cause, without regard for who is the actual perpetrator; and the "missionaries," like Timothy McVeigh, who when interviewed after his conviction for the bombing of the Alfred P. Murrah building in Oklahoma City, said he believed that the whole country believed as he did and only needed someone to "get the revolution started." He *thought* he was a moderate.[29]

Thrill seekers of this kind are probably all just psychopathic. They're unpredicatble and unfocused. There are more of them among the leadites so they should be getting fewer – but they're much better equipped than previous loonies. They care about no one but themselves and pick out any group that's different, just for the hell of it. The other three kinds probably all quite wrongly and quite fervently think the Empire is on their side. The "defenders" are probably all paranoid or at least xenophobic. Retaliators oversimplify and over-compartmentalize people, thinking "they're all like that[30] so what's the difference." The missionaries are the ones most people think all terrorists are. Very few in number but they lie in wait and scheme until they can get the greatest impact. What we need to work out is how to keep them from recruiting the other three, and how to give all these people a sense of agency that involves building rather than destroying.

---

29 That's a big problem with humans: we tend to think that all other people think like we do, until proven otherwise. It's a shame Mr. McVeigh had to detonate a bomb in front of a federal building's daycare to find out how wrong he was.
30 Or all in it together.

THE EMPIRE HAS NO CLOTHES!

Terrorist groups tend to grow out of political and economic anger and then take on a religious face, often to simplify their PR campaign. "Holy war" is easier to sell than "my town was destroyed by a war between A and B, so I'm going to kill C because they should have done something about it, or tried and failed, or tried to help and made it worse, or were friends with A or B at one time in the past. It's easier just to make "everyone else" the enemy, and that plays well into perceptions and delusions of persecution.

That's not to say that the Empires haven't made life harder than it has to be on several fronts. We mostly do our best, and we fail, and sometimes we do harm along the way. When we fail to correct those harmful mistakes, when we don't clean up our messes, we tend to step in them later.

September 11

What led up to 9/11 is on America. Make no mistake, those attacks were inexcusable. America's mistakes don't justify 9/11, but you can't really understand such acts unless you understand why people do them. It didn't just happen in isolation, out of meaningless hatred. There were some necessary causes that pointed that anger at us.

When the Soviet Union first invaded Afghanistan, the Afghans didn't really see an issue with it. America was afraid of the Soviets and wanted the Afghans to be afraid, too, so we made it into a religious war. "The godless Soviets are here to destroy your religion." So the CIA created the Mujaheddin, who fought the Soviets to protect their Islam. Babylon 5's Commander Sinclair said, *"you should never hand a gun to someone unless you're absolutely certain where they're going to point it. Your mistake."* We handed them a gun and made them afraid. When the Soviets left, we left, too. Three months of war costs would have built schools, hospitals, and friends. Instead we just walked away, and they realized they'd been used as pawns in someone else's game. We became no better than the Soviets in their eyes, and probably next to invade. So the Mujaheddin morphed into Al Qaeda, and in the fear we created they pointed the gun we gave them at us. The cost of not making friends has been far higher than the cost of making them would have been. America created the Mujaheddin, used them, and then tossed them aside. We made them fear for their sense of agency so they'd fight the Soviets, and left them with the focus we'd created once they'd done everything we wanted them to. What else could we expect?

So we got drawn into war again. We've been doing better this time. I hope we continue doing better and I hope it works. American policy has a habit of changing with elections, and that tends to leave a lot of loose ends untied.

Is Money Everything?

Everybody eventually asks this question. Most answer "no," and some answer "yes." Those who answer "no" usually disdain and distrust the others, and those who answer "yes" often pity the rest.

I've been pretty well-off and I've been nearly homeless. I've had years where I made six figures and years when my taxable income was negative. I've been robbed, cheated, underpaid, and gone unpaid for good work, and I've been treated well, paid well, and received great generosity when I needed it desperately. I have friends who've fared worse than my worst and better than my best. I know a little about this and I can tell you with some authority that the people who answer this question "yes" are wrong, and those who answer "no" are wrong, too.

How can that be, that both answers can be wrong at the same time? It's simple: it's the wrong question. Like being on a Groucho Marx game show or in front of a Joseph McCarthy board of inquiry, you can't answer the wrong question correctly.

When I was destitute, literally digging change out of the furniture to buy my first meal in three days, (my friend and I ate the taco bar bare) I came to the first part of my realization about this. Having just three dollars and change, right then, was critical. Not having money consumed all my attention and energy; I had nothing left to give to other pursuits. When I'm poor, even a quarter can make a difference. Money is important to the degree that you don't have it.

When I'm wealthy, a few dollars mean nothing. If I lose them, it makes no difference. I'm setting money aside, and if a check is a week late as sometimes happens, it's a minor inconvenience. I'm not living from check to check. Due to having been destitute and other circumstances that have left me with debts to pay, I'm not rich by any first-world standard. I still need to work. Even if I moved out into my very, very old motor home I'd still have regular payments to make on other things, and I think that's really important to the question.

The Poor Trap

My dad used to say that if you're living check to check, if missing one check is an emergency, then you're in the poor trap. If you're in the poor trap it doesn't matter if you make twenty dollars a week or twenty thousand. Which brings me to my next observation, and then on to the answer to the right question.

By my dad's definition, some "wealthy" people are poor, and this is mostly *by choice*. Many of these high cash flow poor-by-choice people then project themselves onto the truly poor and claim that *they* are the ones who are poor by choice instead of admitting to their own problems. Some *and only some* "poor" people aren't – aborigines for example: it's a lot easier to not be poor with no income if you don't have to pay to live on your land.[31] In fact, it's the only way. Some wealthy people are so deathly afraid of being poor that, like Scrooge, they amass great sums of wealth and do nothing with it but hoard. They are terrified of being poor even though there's no rational possibility of that ever happening to them. They live in fear: the same fear that the poor live in, except their fear is completely self-imposed. It's a shame they can't see their own security and live their lives instead of endlessly defending themselves from threats that don't exist.

---

31 This gets into the whole subject of rent, mortgages, and especially property taxes. That would be a book in itself, but suffice it to say that property taxes may be a great driver of perpetual poverty. Certainly they prevent people from getting out of the game and freeing their economic niche for someone else.

THE EMPIRE HAS NO CLOTHES!

The Root of All Evil

Ambition is fine, and if you're like Elon Musk for example and use the proceeds of that ambition to push the limits of what's possible in the interest of making better things for everyone, then that's wonderful. And if you get richer doing it, then as long as everyone involved benefits fairly as well, that's even more wonderful.

Greed isn't the same as ambition. Greed is the irrational need to accumulate more and more for its own sake. Greed is mere collectorism, the desire to always have more because you are incapable of feeling like you have enough. "Dollars - collect the whole set!" It's born one or both of these things:

> A Sauron-like fear of losing even the most miniscule bits of perceived agency. This terror drives a need to have power over all others.

> The abject terror of poverty. This fear and it puts people in a combat mentality. It leads people to try to win, even to cheat, rather than to succeed.

Avarice is born of fear, and it really is the root of nearly all evil.

What Is It, Then?

In all this we find the truth: *wealth isn't everything but poverty is.* So if you're making good money, be sure to pay off your debts and set some aside. There's nothing quite like knowing that if you don't have an income next month you'll be fine.[32]

Survival Instinct

The milder side of greed, and perhaps part of its origin, is collecting. Many people collect things. In the early days of homo sapiens it was

---

32 I used a month of unemployment to write this book. My last paycheck came last week and as I write this I'm beginning to wonder how we'll get through the next couple of months, but at least we're okay right now.

skins, food, tools, and weapons. It was always good to have more than you needed in case something went wrong, and we weren't yet very good at making educated forecasts about the future. So we hoarded food for the winter like squirrels do and amassed a varied collection of knives and spears and spear-throwers. Each just a little different and each better suited to one situation or another, or all the same as the best one so far just in case we lose one or break it or the beast just won't die. As our collections grew, we became not just protective of them but fond of them and intensely fascinated with their application and minor variations. In time we become fond of those things upon which we were dependent. That instinct probably plays a role in infant-parent bonding and in that context it's a very good thing. Turned in the wrong direction it can lead to a level of greed and jealousy that can be very harmful to one's long-term well being, and it can happen with anything we see as "ours." That's probably why most stone-age cultures have (or had) no concept of private property. With so little to go around it was best not to be fighting over which spear was whose in case of a big cat attack. It was ours, and we all took care of it as if all our lives depended on it. Because they did. Five spears might be enough for a village, but one person on his own might need that many. Sharing makes the same amount of stuff go a lot farther. Like car sharing does now. Twenty people who only need cars occasionally can get by sharing one or two. Fractional ownership lets people buy 20% of an airplane without being stuck with one wing, all the seat belts, and two pistons. Sharing makes the expensive stuff go farther.

Gone Bonkers

As our collected wealth grew along with the sums of our games, so did the variety of things we collected.[33] We started with things that had intrinsic value like tools, but that didn't last long: we soon made art and body decorations and other things we could call our own even if we couldn't yet throw the rest of the clan out of "our" cave. Today we

---

33 It occurs to me that money can be a kind of "virtual collection." I could have a thousand glow-in-the-dark elephants, fishing lures, Matchbox cars, or whatever. Maybe for some there's a certain vicarious pleasure in looking at the collections of others and knowing you could afford to own that, so you don't have to.

collect all manner of things including art, real estate, money, and power. It's a survival instinct gone berserk in a situation it's not really tuned for. Anything that even appears to threaten our collection is immediately viewed as a threat. Our view of the world is strongly affected by the size, quality, and number of our collections. The glass cats and glowing elephants carry on their march, sometimes trampling our real lives in the process. Private property makes us *feel* completely independent; yet without "the outside world" to make steel and gasoline and power tools and electricity, most of us would be dead in 60 days. We're still interdependent; it's just that our collections make us feel more insulated. We surround ourselves with stuff in a vain attempt to feel safe. If you really want to feel safe, go to a bank. They have one. A safe, that is.

So people cheat to maintain their collections, be they tools, shelter, money, love, ideas, or any other valuable stuff. We don't like giving up our stuff, and why should we? We're natural born collectors, and even if you're not, nearly everyone around you is. So the next time your boss or coworker or spouse or child fights against what seems like a good idea, find out what they think they'll be losing. Maybe the sum isn't as high as you thought, or maybe you just need to explain to them how you all can win. Of course, this assumes that they will act fairly once they understand, and in some people these instincts are just too strong. At that point it's fair to call them phobias and compulsions.

In older times we collected a dozen or more of the same kind of tool because we never knew which one would have the particular characteristic we'd need to fend off that saber-toothed tiger. Now many of us have the compulsion to "collect the whole set," as if there were some intrinsic value in doing so.

Why Do We Love Our Collections?

In 1964, a number of hostages were taken during a botched bank robbery in Stockholm, Sweden. Over the course of four days, the captives were repeatedly threatened with death only to have their lives spared each time. The hostages quickly began to try to understand their volatile captors and do the things that would keep them happy. Perfectly understandable, since they want to survive and making your captors angry is not a good way to do that. They began to see the world through their captors' eyes. In time, the captives began to see the police as the enemy and actually resisted rescue! Many of the captives spoke and testified in defense of the bank robbers, and one former captive actually married one of them! They had permanently confused their vulnerability and dependency with affection in only four days.

As parents we don't (we'd better not!) threaten our children's lives, but we do make our displeasure known. As children we are well aware of the likes and dislikes of those we depend upon for our lives. Bonding to our parents may take longer than four days, but the conditions are thankfully a lot less intense.

Money!

Economics has been called "the dismal science." I've heard a lot of definitions of economics over the years, but the simplest and most complete is this: "the study of shortages." Any time you have less to go around than you need, you have a shortage of it, and an economy builds around it. It gets a price, and has a cost. People worry about having enough if it, and they worry about others taking it. Dismal science, indeed! Shortages bring out the worst in us, but they also bring out a drive to make things better. To make the shortage go away. If we try to make the shortage go away for everyone, we are good, even noble; but, if we try to make it go away only for ourselves, then we are at best mediocre and at worst bad, greedy, possibly even evil sots depending on how we go about things.

Manufacturing and Service

The Empire talks about the manufacturing sector, service sector, and so on. It's never had a good place to put people who write software. This is the way it was years ago and I don't know if they've ever fixed it. If I write software for a client I'm performing a service. If I write it for a company that puts it on physical media and sells that media, it's manufacturing. Either way I've done the exact same thing the exact same way but it gets accounted differently.

As far as I'm concerned, there are very few primary sectors. If, when you're done, you've made something new that's more than what you

108

started with, you're in the making sector. Making creates wealth by literally creating valuable stuff. Making includes things like manufacturing, building houses, writing software, art, and doing research. You create tools, toys, or knowledge.

If you grow food, produce fuel, clean the restrooms, or fix stuff, you're in the fixing sector. You don't make new things but you keep the things that are there, going. This includes medics, who keep us going.

If you entertain live, cook meals, answer phones, or babysit, you're in the doing sector. The doing sector doesn't create or preserve wealth, but it does redistribute it.

The "service" sector is pretty much the same as the "doing" sector. You can't have a service-based economy that grows. Everyone can't just help each other into prosperity. At some point someone has to make more stuff so that there's more value to go around.

You can break these three sectors down farther, but at its simplest that's it. You either make stuff, keep stuff going, or do stuff. If no one makes stuff, then eventually entropy catches up with you and no one can afford to have stuff fixed any more. Making stuff is very, very important and every economy needs to be doing lots of it or face decline because making is the only real growth. Everything else is built on top of it.

It's hard to measure the impact of the making sector. Things like houses, cars, and other more or less permanent items (very durable goods) result in wealth capture. The money spent for the item gets measured only once, but the impact of that wealth capture on the buyer is vital and long outlasts the transaction. Years later it's no longer measured as part of the domestic product but it has a persistent impact on the economics of its owner.

When the making sector gets it wrong, there can be big problems. Small cars burst into flames. Airplanes fall down. The entire infrastructure of information falls apart. Y2K was piles and piles of expense on top of expense, because a whole lot of stuff wasn't made right in the first place.

THE EMPIRE HAS NO CLOTHES!

Creating Demand

I'll admit that it's possible to make it harder than it has to be to make stuff and making it easier can sometimes encourage more to be made. Still, simply creating something doesn't create a market for it. If that were the case, why would nine out of ten new businesses fail?

Creating the computer didn't create a demand for it. The abacus and the adding machine were proof that a better way of handling numbers was needed. Early computers were hard to use. Only governments and businesses could use them fully. The CEO of IBM said in the 1950s, "I perceive the world market for computers as being about three." And that's about what they sold of those complicated, bulky, expensive, power-hungry, slow, temperature-sensitive behemoths. As computers got smaller and cheaper and began to do more things, people who needed to do those things began buying them. When accountants' large paper spreadsheets were mimicked by VisiCalc on the Apple II, people began to really see how these new machines could *help them do things they were already doing*. Sales exploded. The market, the demand, was already there. It had been there for centuries. VisiCalc and Apple simply realized it. Others followed quickly when they recognized other existing demand they could fulfill.

Cars are the same way. There were already cars before the automobile came along, before gasoline was invented. They were typically one or two horsepower, literally. Horses are expensive and require lots of care, and cleaning up horse-powered cities is a horrible job. Most people can't afford them, so there were coaches for hire. There were taxis long before there were automobiles. Trains had already proven that engines could move people more effectively than animals could. Then Daimler-Benz invented the automobile in 1896. It was hard and complicated to work, expensive, and the hand starter crank was dangerous. Henry Ford changed very little about it, but applied the assembly line to it and made it cheaper than horses. Despite its complexity[34], it caught on. They were cheaper than horses, so more

---

34 It was Cadillac, in 1916, that finally settled on the control arrangement we have today with its Type 53. It took 20 years for someone to get it right!

people could buy them. They took a lot less maintenance than horses, so more people could keep them. They filled a need we'd been trying to fill for thousands of years with horses and boats and trains, even hot air balloons. The demand was always there. It's just that it was filled by other things for quite a long time.

Supply doesn't create demand. Demand creates supply as the car and computer show. For there to be demand, people have to make more than a subsistence wage. They have to have disposable income. When you're living hand-to-mouth, the only thing you can demand is "cheaper!" You can't demand "more" or "better." As soon as you have a living wage you can demand new and better things, and that demand gives someone a chance to make what you want. You have created a job!

A job isn't just an agreement between a provider and a customer. It's an unrealized demand.

The Empire's definition of a job, an arrangement between a provider and a customer, is incomplete. That is the definition of a *realized* or *actual* job. There are a lot of potential jobs out there that haven't been made real yet. There's a lot of demand that isn't being met yet. That unmet demand for work I call *potential jobs*. They exist, if you can recognize them, and can be converted into *actual jobs* simply by doing them!

People hiring people won't create jobs any more than people making things create demand. People wanting things and being able to buy them create demand. Demand creates jobs, which if they pay well enough in turn create more demand which creates more jobs.

Demand creates supply, not the other way around.

Hiring people doesn't create jobs. Paying them well does.

If you simply accumulate jobs, say by bringing in a big-box hardware store and pushing the local shops out of business, you haven't created any jobs even if you hire more people. Especially if you pay those people less. Odds are, though, you pay no more and actually hire fewer people because that's efficient and how you keep your prices down. You're a job destroyer.

THE EMPIRE HAS NO CLOTHES!

You *might* create some jobs downstream if the people who save money in your store use that money to buy other stuff they wouldn't have before, but *don't* count your employees as jobs created. They're jobs accumulated or jobs realized.

It gets really hard, then, to know when jobs are actually created, but it's easy to tell when they're realized. When the Empire says, "the economy created 100,000 new jobs last month," what it means is, "the economy *realized* 100,000 jobs last month." We have no way of knowing how many were created or destroyed, though if there's a net wage loss, we can be sure that jobs were destroyed.

We Need More Pillars!

Without pillars there's no roof, and without a roof it's hard to sleep when it rains. For most of my life, the Michigan economy has stood on four pillars: automobiles, office furniture, tourism, and agriculture. The first three are all good-times businesses. When times are bad, people don't travel. They don't need new office furniture (there are a dozen unused chairs in conference room 3). They don't buy new cars, but keep the ones they've already paid off. When the US economy changes, Michigan's changes more. In good times, Michigan rides on top. In bad times, it's on the bottom. To change that means bringing in more kinds of business, and a lot of each.

In years when the crops are bad, or tourism is down, Michigan is down. The failure of any one pillar might bring down the house. Any two pillars **will** bring it down. If the failure of one pillar can bring down our economic house, then the first woodpecker on the scene will doom us all. A roof should be held up at so many points that even if a quarter of them get taken out by woodpeckers the roof will still stand. While we figure out how to frighten off woodpeckers. "Too big to fail" is too big to be allowed. More pillars!

The Real Driver

Michigan's economy taught me something else. The Empire says that consumer spending is responsible for two thirds of private economic activity. I think that's wrong: consumer spending is responsible for <u>all</u> of it. Why? Because there would be no business-to-business demand if not for consumer spending. My business won't buy stuff or rent space from your business if I'm not selling anything. *Business spending is just a consumer spending multiplier.*

Consumer confidence <u>is</u> the economy. Fear stays home and hoards cash but confidence travels on credit. You can talk about all the other economic "fundamentals," but consumer confidence is more powerful than any of them. When people spend money they create jobs and that's a self-reinforcing cycle up to the natural output of that economy. Even beyond, if you can invent new stuff.

Money Can't Buy Happiness

I remember a study that was done. Yes, another study. Study your studies. This one asked three questions of people, and the results are something the Empire doesn't like to talk about because it's invested in other myths. The questions were simple: how happy are you now, how much do you make, and how much would you need to make to be completely happy. The answer to the third question was about the same for everyone. Living on welfare, just starting a career with nothing in savings, any tier of middle class, top 10%, top 1%, top 0.1% - they all said the same thing. To be completely happy they needed about 15% more than they made now.

So guess what! Since everyone gave the same answer, we see that money doesn't buy happiness.

Except that it does... to a point. Remember I said that wealth isn't everything, but poverty is? That first question is big. As a group, poor people are remarkably unhappy. When people have some disposable income and a little in savings, they become lots happier. It's that agency thing again: they have some control, some power over their lives at that point. Beyond that the effects of more money drop off quickly. At a certain level of wealth, and it was under $200,000 a year if I recall correctly, more money does absolutely nothing to make you happier, even though people believe it will.[35]

Money Can't Buy Time

No? Ask anyone who's retired. All that retirement time, that pure agency over their time, is bought with saved money. Ben Franklin said, "time is money." It appears to work both ways: money is time. If A=B then B=A. The simple algebra of life. Save money early and often, but don't deny yourself the moments along the way. Live, and pay yourself first. You'll thank yourself later, and it's always fun to have good reason to say, "you're welcome" to yourself.

Okay, well, it can't buy you another day on this Earth! Wrong again. Good health care is expensive. Good housing is costly, as is good food. All of these things increase your lifespan. Money does buy you time. Poverty steals if from you.

The rich live longer and can do with their time precisely what they please. The rest of us can't, so here's my definition of being rich: enough resources to have full agency over your own time without detriment to others. I'd love to have this myself, and live in a world where everyone did. Star Trek's matter replicators made that life possible for them. I hope that some similar technology will one day make shortages a thing of the past for us.

"Won't you beam me somewhere, Mister Scott? Any old place here on Earth or in space. You pick the century and I'll pick the spot."

- Jimmy Buffett

When you have enough money you can spend the rest of your life doing whatever you want to do. Most of us will play, and by that I mean we will set ourselves artificial, arbitrary goals and try to meet them.

---

35 Happiness even drops off *very slightly* as incomes become greater. In "The Paradox of Choice" psychologist Barry Schwartz makes a good case for how the same thing happens sometimes with some choices. Too few are a problem, more is better, but after a point, more actually lead to paralysis and dissatisfaction. Could be that these two things are one in the same, or both driven by "opportunity cost" thinking.

Millions of people doing that are going to find ways around a whole bunch of problems we struggle with today. There are a couple of businesses I'd love to start if I had the resources to do it. If I knew that my daughter wouldn't starve because I tried. America's social safety net is almost good at that, but resources are better. That's why crowdfunding is one of the best things ever in recorded history.

We in the US could crowdfund a lot of things, things we aren't aware of yet, while improving the safety net and saving money. Most people, given safety, will do very interesting things, and some of those will spawn new industries. So, what if we simplified the individual tax code a bit? Here's a kind of broad brush concept. We set the individual income tax rate at something like 25% for everyone. I don't think that income from work should be taxed more than income from wealth, so this is on all income - capital gains, dividends, everything, so the capital gains rate comes up from 15-20%. The bottom 50% pay only 3% of the total income taxes so we can just leave them out. To do that, every adult citizen gets a personal credit of 25% of the $30,500 median income, or $7,625. Now here's the twist: the credit isn't managed by your employer, or your clients, or any other such people. It simply comes to you in the form of a monthly, non-taxable refund check.

So instead of $7 trillion in taxable income, there's $10 trillion. The government pays back $2.5 trillion. No more individual tax returns, except for self-employment and some other circumstances, and a much-loathed federal agency gets cut substantially. Of course, the tax preparers won't like it, but they can take on corporate customers.

For a median married household, the new net income tax would be 25% of (57,000 − 61,000), or negative $1,000 a year. So much for the so-called "marriage tax!" By $130,000 it's 13% and by about half a million it reaches within a hair of 25%. It'll come pretty close to the current $1.8 trillion at much lower administrative cost and a lot less pain to the taxpayers. Employers have a much easier time working out payroll taxes and states' unemployment compensation burdens drop. It'll also take a lot of the weight off people making minimum wage and give them a few more upward options.

THE EMPIRE HAS NO CLOTHES!

"Some people will take the opportunity to just 'drop out.'" Really? For $635 a month? People who would do that, are people who would anyway and probably have already. People who will avoid work at any cost. They're fewer than the Empire would have you think, and do you really want to have them in the work force anyway? The lion's share of the people will use the safety net to improve their agency and their lives, just as they do now - the difference being that the self-employed would share in that safety net. We don't generally qualify for unemployment and this would go a long way in helping people start their own businesses and keep going or retool in lean times. A tax rate of 30%, roughly the rate for much of the upper middle class, would raise the safety net by 20% to $762 or $1524/month for a couple. In a lot of places that would pay the rent or mortgage and utilities, and basic food. In a lot of other places it wouldn't, but it would help a lot.

This could reduce quite a few other subsidies and make retraining, going back to school, and just plain rural living more viable in our rapidly changing economy. It won't pay everything. It's not a living income, not even a basic one, but it would help and save people a lot of money and effort and anguish dealing with their income taxes and help people who choose to live with their aging parents a little more money to deal with it. Combined with Social Security (which the people already paid for and are only getting back later), this could really make a difference for economy and federal budget as a whole. If we can then tweak our other social programs to eliminate the "cliffs" where people lose more in support than they gain in income, we may really have something there.

All Taxation Is Theft!

Or all private property is theft. It depends on who you talk to. Taxation is the state taking your money from you. Ideally it does that to fulfill obligations it has to you: to "establish justice, ensure domestic tranquility, provide for the common defense, promote the general welfare, and secure the blessings of liberty to ourselves and our posterity."

If only we agreed on what all those things meant it would be easy! There we go on agreeing again.

There are those who see that one person greedily hoarding resources diminishes us all, and that's true. We already know that sharing makes the expensive stuff go farther. What one person can't afford, maybe five or ten can. What one person hides away, others can't use to good effect. That leads to an opposite, equally extreme idea: "All private property is theft!"

If all taxation is theft, and all private property is theft, then there is nothing but theft. Collective economies are wonderful things, but they don't scale all that well. Get too many people involved and unfairness, cheating, and conflict will result. Just as they do in capitalist and centrally-controlled economies. It's too bad, too, because some of those non-capitalist systems have awesome ideals at their core.

So if they can't both be right, which one is?

Neither.

THE EMPIRE HAS NO CLOTHES!

Everyone has something in every government budget to disagree with, but defense, police, courts, prisons, public health and safety, business regulation, environmental protection, and quite a few other services are absolutely necessary. We will disagree about *how much* of each might be appropriate, but they're all necessary to protect the nation from its enemies – and the people from crime and abuse by those more powerful and/or less ethical. Taxation isn't theft; it's part of a social contract. We can lament its necessity, but anarchy is neither safe nor stable,[36] and it's not good for anyone.

The fact is that sharing extends the wealth of individuals, and private property does, too. They're both good for the bee and for the hive. If there were no private property, no reward for all that hard work, almost no one would build the stuff that went into the industrial revolution. That revolution would take a lot longer. The material sum of our lives would be a lot less and 80% of us would still be farmers. And there would be about a tenth as many of us. That car you share, that plane or boat you own 10% of, that MP3 player you listen to, this book... none of it would exist yet. Life would be simpler, quieter, and harder.

An important part of taxation is the people having some kind of say in what's done with it. That's why taxation without representation, one of the key problems leading to the American Revolution, is a bad thing. Without representation, the social contract is broken. Right now we're losing that representation in America as monied interests buy more and more influence. As large, unelected corporations grow more powerful than states, they pit one state against another to bargain away all their taxes. We're heading for an America, a world, in which corporations pay no taxes at all and individuals bear the entire load. Those corporations and other monied interests use their money to buy the time and attention of our governing officials, and leave less of it for us. How we get that attention back from the oligarchy is a different chapter and it involves changing something we've done the same way for centuries.

---

36 "Cloak of Anarchy" by Larry Niven is a fun read.

Verbs Make Me Tense

One of the biggest Empires is the Empire of Language. It was said that Socrates could lead anyone to any conclusion simply by asking questions. Groucho Marx used loaded questions for humorous effect: "have you stopped beating your wife" has no safe answer within the frame it's asked! "No" might mean you never did it in the first place and so couldn't stop something you never started, but would be taken as "I still do and I'm proud of it." Senator McCarthy used the same tactics to destroy people and advance his own political ambitions. "Have you given up your membership in the Communist Party" was a favorite of his, and unlike Groucho, who simply caught people off guard, McCarthy bullied people until they gave him the yes or no answer he wanted and cut them off before they could answer fully. Extremism in defense of liberty *is a vice.*

Experiments in controlled settings show that language doesn't affect problem solving. Experiments in controlled settings also show that nearly every child over about four years of age will always pass a "theory of mind" test. It goes like this. Jim and Lisa are in a room with a table and two boxes marked one for each of them. Lisa puts her lunch in her box, closes it, and leaves the room. Jim takes Lisa's lunch out of her box, puts it in his own box, and closes both boxes. Lisa comes back to get her lunch. Which box does she look in to find it?

Simple: she looks in her box *because she doesn't know something that Jim does.* The understanding that other people have different knowledge is

119

called "theory of mind." In a test setting we pass every time because we're paying attention to that. In everyday life, though, we often assume that people know things they don't, or don't know things that they do, because we don't actually know what they know. We fail what's called *spontaneous* theory of mind tests every day of our lives. Some of us more than others. What's obvious to one is arcane, even occult to others. Yet we assume that because we all looked at the same thing, we all *saw and understood* the same thing. We don't.

I'm Not Tense

Language is a lot like that. We all speak the same language, but we don't. Or we speak different languages. It affects us and the way we make decisions. In laboratory settings language doesn't affect problem-solving ability, but in spontaneous situations it does. Here's one small example. Not as small as a Hamster, but small.

Some languages don't have verb tense. The language doesn't support the construct of past, present, or future for a verb. You have to get it from the context in the rest of the sentence. People whose first language doesn't have verb tense can speak only in the present, then modify that with a noun for the time frame. Danish has a past tense but no future tense in most cases.

In English we would say, " I will need this money in 20 years."

In Danish we would say, "I need this money, 20 years from now."

In English we say, "I will need this," and we tend to put off saving because we don't need it now.

In Denmark they are much, much better at saving for the future. "I need this," so they set it aside now, because now is now. The language you speak, and the way you speak it, really does change the way you act. Your words create your future by shaping how you act in the present.

It's the End of the World as We Know It

And I feel fine!

If the life you want to live really does determine what you believe, then what does that say to me about some very pessimistic movements?

There are people who believe that the end is upon us because Jesus is returning and "soon" means in their lifetimes. So far, "soon" has been just shy of 2,000 years. If 2,000 years can be "soon" in God's eyes, then 2,000 more can still be soon. They can't accept that. Why? Probably because many of them want to act however they please without worrying about the world they leave for their children. They want a life where the long-term consequences of their actions don't exist, because there's no such thing as long-term consequences. It's psychopathic. We need a longer view because it's very likely that our great-to-the-thousandth grandchildren are going to have to live here.

The self-declared "Islamic State" is the same thing only worse. Its people not only want the world to end, they want to enjoy killing other people to make it happen. That's one way to avoid facing long-term consequences: kill everyone who disagrees with you and delude yourself into believing it's a good thing. So they believe themselves the instruments of Allah's will when in fact they're nothing but a bunch of mass murderers out for a thrill and cherry picking their beliefs to match. It's a good thing that their kind are on a short list for extinction.

There are probably some doomsday preppers who actually prep out of fear and self-defense, but I think that most of them — without even knowing it — believe that civilization is going to fall because they feel oppressed by the very existence of society and want the life of agency and power that they think they'll live when social order falls.[37] Many of them are people who see their rural lifestyle falling to urbanization, and that probably reinforces their sense of desperation. Prepping is the only power they feel they have left.

Kind of explains the long popularity of Westerns, doesn't it? A lot of people want to live in a world like that. They prefer the option of being able to kill their oppressors over a safe and orderly life for their children that offers them challenges they don't enjoy facing. The problem is, that other world never exists for long. It can't because it's unstable. A strong government is, unfortunately, a necessity. Let's make sure it does good, noble, and occasionally very cool things.

Star Trek gave us an a very different view of "the end of the world *as we know it*" because their matter replicators brought an end to shortages. All you need is a cheap and abundant supply of energy and an equal mass and you've got whatever you need. Got a rock but really need a steak dinner? No problem. At the point where all your physical needs are guaranteed to be met, then agency is no longer an issue and you are truly free and can find your own goals to pursue. Goals that have nothing to do with "need" and everything to do with "better."

---

37 I'll admit that social expectations can be quite a burden, and I'm delighted to have grown up largely oblivious to them. You can learn to ignore them if you want to!

Moral Direction, Not Peer Pressure

Long ago, if you acted badly you were kicked out of the tribe and probably eaten by something larger and more powerful than yourself, or you simply starved or died of dysentery like so many of the mountain men of the American west. In the cities, religion was used as the opiate of the masses to keep them in line. The state had the power of death and the church would have you believe it held the keys to eternal life. That immense carrot and stick combination made the church the power behind the throne for centuries in much of the world and kept the people cowed.

We don't have any of that any more, and as you can tell I think that's a good thing. It's clear that we have more agency than at any time in civil history. Match that with two decades of falling crime and violence in those parts of the world that banned lead from gasoline, and it's clear that we've got a pretty nice world to live in.

What's not so clear is this: how do we maintain a sense of right and wrong without that social pressure? Let's go back and play some games.

A Negative-Sum Game is a game in which all players can lose because once the game is over there is less to go around.

A Zero-Sum Game is a game in which some players must lose if any are to win because there is nothing actually gained in its playing: there's the same amount of stuff at the end as there was in the beginning.

A Positive-Sum Game is a game in which all players can win because

THE EMPIRE HAS NO CLOTHES!

there is more stuff after the game is played than there was before.

This is pretty obvious once you think about them, and now we can play even more. Games are better when there are rules, so let's find some. We all need to know the rules before we start to play. That's one way the Empire has really let us down because too many of the rules are unspoken and unwritten. Calvinball was fun to read about in *Calvin and Hobbes*, but playing it for real would be even more annoying than it was for Hobbes.

Rule 1: Avoid Negative-Sum Games. Any time you can just not play one of these games, everyone is better off. As the computer in the movie "War Games" said, "Strange game. The only winning move is not to play." War is the most dramatic example of a negative-sum game. Don't start them.

Rule 2: Avoid Zero-Sum Games. Simply put, they're not worth the effort and it's no good to be on the losing end. When it's all over, if anyone wins it's probably theft. Gambling and fraud are zero-sum games.

Rule 3: Play Positive-Sum Games. Play lots of them. Play the ones with the most positive sums, the ones that create the most new "stuff." These are the games that have no losing end. Everybody wins.

Rule 4: Play fairly, distributing the risks and rewards proportionately among the players and not subjecting any player to more risk than he is willing to accept.

Rule 5: Not everyone values the same things you do in the same way you do, so be sure to ask. Informed consent is vital. You don't want your agency violated by people playing on your lawn without your permission, and they don't want you to do that to them.

My Code

I've written a lot of code. Millions of lines of it over the years. Most of it's still running. My stuff from the 1980s passed Y2K reviews a decade later without change. But that's not what this is about.

You who are on the road / must have a code / that you can live by

This is Crosby, Stills, and Nash code, not Alan Turing code. Except I won't be singing. You'll thank me for that.

Definitions – The Boring Part

What I want to talk about here is really simple. So simple that I understood it so intuitively that it took me 15 years to find the words. I found them more than 15 years ago when my daughter first looked up at me and asked, "why." It's amazing – my two year old had been keeping my words hidden away for all those years!

I never found a publisher for "Ethics In Our Universe." I considered self-publishing, and the then-tiny ebook market. It sat there for another 15 years. I re-edited it at least half a dozen times and was never happy. This section is part of that old book, and it's gonna read like it.

The problem with talking about stuff this fundamental is that darned High Llama. Like the little man on the stair[38], he's everywhere when I

---

38 "I saw a man upon the stair, a little man who was not there. He was not there again today. Gee, I wish he'd go away."

talk about ethics, so before I can tell you my words, I have to tell you what a bunch of my words mean. They're not the legal definitions, they're mine.

Distress is anything which will result in harm if continued, but will not cause harm if immediately terminated, as in sleep or food deprivation.

Harm can be physical, mental, or structural. Every kind of harm requires that the effect be enduring, lasting after the cause is removed and initial aid is rendered.

Physical harm is any increase in entropy or the capacity to export it, as with starvation, cold, injury, or disease. One symptom of harm is a reduction in physical capacity, either temporary or permanent.

Mental harm is any decrease in the ability of the mind to make risk assessments, judge the sum of a game, decide the best games, make plans to play them, or execute these plans. This includes emotional problems which cloud judgment or inhibit mental function.

Structural harm is harm to or removal of any of the possessions, systems, society, or individuals which support an individual's ability to provide for the needs of itself and those under its authority. More simply, it's a denial of agency that creates a threat of other harm.

Help is anything which: improves health or otherwise undoes or mitigates a past harm; protects from immediate or future harm; reduces the probability of harm; improves the ability to take and manage risk; gives comfort; or provides needed information.

Negligence is the failure to explore and evaluate foreseeable risks and obtain informed consent. It is not the failure to foresee everything. Humans aren't perfect and can't be expected to be perfect fortune tellers.

Gross Negligence is the failure to make any effort to look for risks or evaluate known risks. To act without thinking is gross negligence.

All Affected goes far beyond "all participants." It covers everyone who may be affected by direct or indirect effects, whether foreseen or

126

unforeseen.

Informed Consent isn't just recognition or fatalistic acceptance of risks, but active, spoken, willing agreement to participate in or be affected by an act, after first being provided with as complete, accurate and truthful information as is available about the sum of the game, all potential for harm and help, and the responsibilities of all involved to preserve or increase the sum and manage risks.

Proclamations – The Grandiose Part

Okay, we're done with the boring part. Now you know what my words mean, so here they come. Duck![39]

There are acts that are right, acts that are wrong, and acts which are neither.

No one has the right to do wrong.

Everyone has the right to do right.

No one has the right to prevent another from doing right.

An act is wrong if it causes harm, increases the risk of harm, or is intended to do harm, without the informed consent of all affected.

An act is right *if it is not wrong* and it: improves health or otherwise undoes or mitigates a past harm; protects from immediate harm; reduces the probability of harm; gives comfort; or provides needed information.

Put simply:

"First, do no harm. Then seek the greatest good for the greatest number, keeping everyone informed and getting consent, and spread the risks and rewards fairly."

It's a variation on European Utilitarianism. Imhotep said, "First, do no harm" more than a thousand years before Hippocrates, but because "Imhotepic Utilitarianism" rolls off the tongue like poisoned sandpaper with thorns, I call my code *Hippocratic Pragmatism*. I try never to say "expialidocious" after it, but it doesn't always work.

---

39 Yes, I know, it's a fowl thing to say, but I'm quacking up here.

THE EMPIRE HAS NO CLOTHES!

Always ask yourself and others if this is the best that can be done.

Never assume that others value the same things in the same way you do. Always get the informed consent of everyone affected – that way you know for sure.

Always be on the lookout for a higher sum, not just for yourself but for all affected.

Always ask yourself whether any change in plans changes the balance of risks and rewards.

Always inform everyone of any new risks or rewards you become aware of.

Always reward the players in proportion to their risks and compensate for any harm. The entrepreneur who mortgaged her home gets paid before the venture capitalist who bet a fraction of the money he could already afford to lose.

Always let people make their own decisions. They know their situation and risk tolerance far better than you do, just as you know these things about yourself better than anyone else.

Always be on the lookout for risks, especially in situations where your consent is received by social contract.

Never punish anyone for being honest, or for harm you suffered due to your own negligence.

Never take more than your fair share.

Never take anything without receiving informed consent.

Never keep relevant secrets from affected people. An exception might be a surprise party where keeping the secret actually increases the sum (in this case joy) of the person being deceived.

Never lie to anyone about anything. This doesn't mean being "brutally honest." You can be tactful and still be honest. If your wife asks if you think she's lost weight and you're just not in the mood to try to judge or answer, then say so. Saying "this isn't a good time to ask" is far better

128

than lying. "I don't know but you look good to me" is also a very good answer. Also, you can't get informed consent if you're misinforming people. Finally, there are ties when you have to keep a secret. "I'm not going to tell you that" is an honest answer.

Never ask a question you don't want answered. This goes along with never lie to anyone. Let me share the moment that illustrates it well. My (now) wife and I were shopping for a wedding dress. She tried one on and asked:

"Does this dress make me look fat?"

"That question isn't fair to me," I said. "It turns a judgment of the dress into a judgment of you. No matter what my answer is today, at some point I'm going to have to either lie to you or hurt your feelings."

She thought about it for a moment. "I see what you mean. Does this dress make me look good?"

"Better," I said, "but the same problem."

A moment. "Do you like this dress on me?"

"I love it." She always stuck to the third question after that. I gotta recommend that if you do this, do it when you can close with "I love it."

Be positive – it's good for you.

The more people you affect, the more responsibility you have. Count the number of people affected. Multiply this by the responsibility you have when taking actions or making decisions that affect only yourself.

Remember that the more power you have, the more people you work for. It's not the other way around, as the many in the Empire would like you to think.

Treat other people's property better than you treat your own. Remember that more people are affected. If you're renting it's not just you and the landlord, but your neighbors and the yet-unknown renters who will follow you who may be affected.

THE EMPIRE HAS NO CLOTHES!

Self-Defense

Better than self-offense, I guess. I try never to attack me or offend myself. It works most of the time.

If you think you're defending someone, first decide if it's something that offends you personally or if there really is a harm being done or threatened. Is the harm only going to hurt the one posing the threat, or is someone else at risk?

If the threat is purely to the actor, point out the danger to him.

If not...

Find a way of preventing immediate and, if possible, future harm.

Take advantage of all social structures, including police and safety in numbers. Sometimes simply moving to a well-lit, crowded street is enough to protect you.

Don't transfer risks to others without their consent. Police have agreed in advance to give their consent by virtue of their position as police, so don't be afraid to ask for their help. Policing is a noble pursuit, and most police serving good governments are noble people. Give them their chance.

Use only as much force as is necessary to guarantee an adequate defense. That usually means using more force than is being used on the victim, so be careful that the force used in defense is justified by the threat. Don't shoot pickpockets, just tackle (or video) them and have them arrested.

Deadly force is certainly justified to defend against potentially deadly force. Not necessarily required or encouraged, merely justified. Be very certain that the threat is in fact potentially deadly because deadly force, even when justified, can't be undone. Some say that killing in self-defense lowers you to the level of your would-be murderer. I say "poppycock." The person who unilaterally decides that someone is going to die this day, should be the one to do so. Remember that the attacker is forcing a negative-sum game on the victim, while the defender is trying to prevent it. Anyone who starts a negative-sum game has no moral right to complain (or sue!) if they lose. They set the rules and forced them on you. Their choice, not yours.

War and other Combat Situations

The Empire's clothes change fast in war. Congress got mad at France for not allowing our warplanes to cross the full breadth of their country on their way to a fight the French wanted no part of and suddenly a whole list of things France "didn't invent" spread far and wide. French fries were renamed "freedom fries" in the House commissary by order of the House of Representatives.

Then there are the cases where people *knowingly* play negative-sum games with people they believe have done the same to them. This is called *revenge* and is probably the most common wrong thing we humans choose to do. Revenge is a negative-sum game. It has to be, because the objective is to do harm for the sake of doing harm. By both of these definitions it's obviously wrong, even if directed at the "right" person. What's worse is that revenge just begets revenge and the sum spirals down and down as more and more people get dragged into it. Eventually you end up with a war in which no one can really remember the causes because everyone knows someone who's been harmed and it's become personal, a war not of conquest and defense but of revenge upon revenge. Wars that become revenge games can drag on for centuries. Look at the Israeli/Arab problem and the former English/Irish problem, just to name two. Similar problems brought waves of war, even genocide, to millennia of recorded history.

All Wars Are Wrong

Let's be honest: if there weren't wrong being done there would be no war. We fight wars to stop wrongs and we launch wars that are just plain wrong themselves. Either way, whoever started it is wrong, whether they fired the first shot or incited it. All wars are wrong, but that's only half the story.

All wars are wrong, but not all who fight in them are wrong. To start a war is to force a negative-sum game upon others. Defending yourself in war is protecting yourself and your family and others. You can fight in a war and be very, very right; but war is never a good thing. It's always bad, and we should avoid it when we can. Those who are right in war should be very careful not to fall into the old revenge game.

What made the U.S. campaign in Afghanistan after September 11th different from revenge? It's subtle, but important. The United States struck back at those who had attacked it, not for the purpose of simply hitting back, but for the purpose of preventing further attacks on innocents. People who only understood violence and revenge were treated to something they could not possibly have understood. The U.S. did not set out to inflict civilian casualties in similar or greater numbers, but it set out to destroy the bastards' ability to kill more people. True, that required killing a great many people belonging to the group that started that particular game, but the strikes were conducted in a way designed to remove their illegitimate stranglehold on the country in which they had sought refuge years before. In the course of that campaign, Afghanistan was lifted back out of the stone age with ordnance and food. Its people were once again allowed to govern themselves and make their own decisions. They were no longer under threat of prison or death simply for sharing ideas, violating a dress code, or having the wrong amount of facial hair.

It's been a long road since I wrote that paragraph in 2003, and things still aren't wonderful there – but they are a lot better. It would have been good if the U.S. had much sooner played a more active role in the rebuilding of the nation, rather than simply protecting the nation-builders from the U.N. and E.U. and more or less leaving it up to them, and eventually we did get more involved. Still, as a collaborative effort it raised millions of people out of the negative-sum game being forced upon them. The campaign punished a wrong, prevented further wrongs,[40] gave comfort to Americans, Afghans, and citizens around the world, and restored a positive-sum life to millions.

Jolly good show. It's a shame that we dropped the ball on the endgame when the Russians were there in the 1980s. Back then we had the opportunity to create allies and friends by building hospitals, schools, and the like. The first time we didn't do it planted the seeds of the second time. A few billion dollars then, just three months of war costs, would have saved us from 9/11 and the ensuing Afghan war. We're finally doing it this time and it's been very expensive, but it does seem to be helping.

The day the statue of Saddam came down I was in Dearborn, MI, the largest Iraqi expatriate population in the world at the time. The celebration was amazing. Just because I was an American I was a national hero to them. In the midst of the speeches, sermons, and parties, I asked how long we had before our forces overstayed our welcome. A face previously covered with great joy turned to sadness and then sympathy. "I don't think you can avoid it." And so it is: any time you win a war on someone else's land, especially if you have to do it without their permission, you end up being an occupying force, and you eventually become the enemy. But if you leave too soon, the trouble you drove out becomes doubled and you take the blame for that. Some wars you just can't win, but we've taken them on anyway for the greater good.

It's been said that America is great because America is good, and that's the whole of it. America isn't great because it's powerful – it's great because of how it uses that power. The day we pull back from the table, quit leading the world's diplomacy, and look inward to our own interests with minimal or no regard for the interests of the rest of the world, America will no longer be great. That will be a sad day.

---

40 How much is something we can never know.

Rules of War

There are those who believe that there are no rules in war, or that the very concept of "Rules of War" is an oxymoron. Not true, as the rise of terrorism in the world clearly illustrates. Terrorists tend to operate outside the accepted rules of war, intentionally targeting non-combatants as a matter of policy.

Unfortunately, we need a military, but contrary to what the Empire would have you think, and rather ironically, a smaller military might actually make us safer. America is the top dog, and a lot of people naturally want to replace the top dog. There will always be those who will be angry at the top dog, simply because it's the top. Whether it's Star Wars, Die Hard, Independence Day, or The Lord of the Rings, we make a lot of movies about the little guy standing up to and defeating a vastly superior force. Well, guess what: to a world where we outspend most countries by a factor of twenty-five or more and operate by far the largest and most advanced air, land, and sea forces in the world, we *are* the Empire to their Rebel Alliance. We don't see ourselves that way, but according to former CIA field officer Amaryllis Fox,[41] a lot of the little guys do. Everyone's fighting for the right reasons in their own eyes, and the only way to disarm your enemy is to listen. When your enemy is a subhuman psychopath who will attack you no matter what you do, the conversation is over and the fighting never will be. But if you listen to your enemy, hear out their policy concerns, and then you've got a chance because your enemy now is a policy. There's a point of work. If all you do is kill people who believe they're fighting for the right reasons, for their children or to end an occupation or a damaging policy, then you might just be "throwing kerosene on a candle" as Fox says. Instead of beating them down, we might try finding out what makes their recruits feel so powerless and do something about that. But how do we make them trust our motives as we change gears?

Scaling back and intervening less should be seen as a reassuring move by those who see us as threatening their national or cultural agency, and

---

41 https://www.youtube.com/watch?v=7WEd34oW9BI

an opportunity to open up a dialog where we do some real listening. For example, if no unfriendly navy has even two aircraft carriers, does America really need eleven nuclear-powered supercarriers (10 in service, 1 in reserve, and 2 under construction)? Why spend so much of our money on them? Even with Russia and China rising (still just one each), twelve is a lot. We can afford to delay the replacement of a couple of these.

The Empire, in the form of a perfect storm of corporate and political ambitions, wants you to think that America's military has grown weak or fallen behind. It's happened in every election cycle I've seen. Think about this, though:[42] America's 611.2 billion spent on its military in 2015 is more than the next nine countries combined, and more than one third of the total global expenditure. It's more than China, Russia, Saudi Arabia, India, France, the United Kingdom, Japan, Germany, and South Korea all rolled together with nearly 20 billion to spare. The next on the list is Italy, and at 27.9 billion it comes in at less than 4% of America's budget. Every other country spends less than that. The remaining 190 countries in total spend just 79% as much as America does by itself.

If that doesn't make America the Empire in military matters, nothing does, and that makes a lot of people and countries around the world feel like Han Solo. If we don't build down and emphasize diplomacy instead of might to help reassure our neighbors, can I at least have a star destroyer?

---

42 Source: SIPRI 2017 Fact Sheet

Competition and Cooperation

John Nash's discovery of Game Theory taught us a funny thing. The way to succeed is always the same: **work together.**

The American Empire worships competition. Get too cooperative and the Empire screams "colllusion" or "conspiracy" or "communism" or "sex!" Our Empire fears cooperation. It's right to, but not so much as it does. The Empire everywhere fears its subjects, and with good reason. Subjects like to change things, and empires don't.

It's funny, though, for all the worship of competition, the examples the Empire gives us are all about greater cooperation. Even in its new clothes, the Empire admits that its old clothes are the real deal.

Cooperation certainly can lead to collusion and conspiracy. Some observers can't tell the difference, but don't let them distract you. Cooperation is the real goal. The problem is that when everyone is working together, some people get lazy and some others get greedy and most of us stop striving to make things better. That's where competition comes in: if I cooperate with my customers better than you do, I'm likely to succeed better than you. You don't want to fail (notice I didn't say 'lose'), so you try harder to improve your cooperation – your products and service – with your customers.

Competition, done right, breeds cooperation along other lines, and it's a great thing. Just don't ever lose sight of the fact that cooperation is still the goal.

THE EMPIRE HAS NO CLOTHES!

Once in a great while, turning rivalry from combat into competition on another field can produce something wonderful. Even as the nuclear powers fought a proxy war in the jungles and rice fields of Viet Nam, they also raced to achieve something greater. That race culminated in the Apollo moon landings of 1969-1972 when for the first time creatures born on this world actually set foot upon another.

We do try to turn wars and rumors of wars into positive-sum games. Sometimes we fail, and sometimes we succeed grandly. Often we do a bit of both. The Empire seems to have a hard time deciding which is more fun: killing people or flying to the moon. Personally I much prefer the moon.

MINE!

Our language frames the way we think of things, especially in spontaneous situations. Controlled laboratory experiments tell us this isn't so, but controlled laboratory experiments also tell us that no one over the age of four or five will ever fail a "theory of mind" test. Yet we have ample proof that people fail them in spontaneous situations all the time. "How could you miss something so obvious!" I'm worse at this than most: because of my Asperger Syndrome I think in moving pictures. I often see those things overlaid on what my eyes see. I can have an idea that I see as a thing in a place in real space. The rest of my experience of the idea is pretty much like yours, I expect, but I actually **see** the thing that "gives" me the idea. Until I realized that, I always expected that everyone else saw that same thing – and that the realization that thing brought was "obvious." Yeah, not. Now I tend to "over-communicate," but at least I don't count on you seeing everything I do. Mostly.

People whose first language lacks verb tense are better at preparing for the future than others. Every language has problems, and those problems constrain the way people look at things. English is particularly poor at expressing relationships through noun forms.

My car, my wife, my dog, my country, my idea.

We call this the "possessive" form in English. I call that rubbish. The word "my" has very different meaning in each of these cases. With thanks to Martin L. Shoemaker, I'll use little subscript letters to help keep them separate here.

139

THE EMPIRE HAS NO CLOTHES!

My$_O$ car. I *own* it. I can keep it, sell it, scrap it, run it off a cliff, shoot holes in it, or let it set in a field for 20 years. I have no responsibility to it. For a slave, "my$_P$ master" is an ownership form in reverse.

My$_F$ wife. We live together by mutual decision. We have responsibilities to each other, and either can end the relationship at any time. I must keep my end up, keep my promises, and fulfill my duties. There is an oath of *fealty*, of reciprocity. The same kind of form as "my$_F$ friend."

My$_R$ dog. A different kind of *relationship*. I have much more say in where the dog lives and how she lives, and I have responsibilities to her.

My$_M$ country. I don't own it, and for the most part it doesn't own me. It certainly doesn't live with me. I am a *member* of it. I identify with it, but it isn't "mine" in the sense that I own it. I wish the language supported these things, because then we could know one another's minds better, at least some of the time. Some say "she's my$_O$ wife," but we all hear "she's my$_F$ wife." We could spot these kinds of problems a lot sooner if the language supported the concepts properly.

When electing representatives, the difference between "my$_M$ country" and "my$_R$ country" or "my$_O$ country" could be critical, but the English language makes no distinction.

The next time someone says, "my" something, think about how they say it and which "my" was spoken. Was it the same "my" you heard? Are you sure? It's not my$_?$ Empire, after all.

I wonder if psychopathy may sometimes be the state of seeing every "my" I say as my$_O$ or at least my$_R$ and everyone else's "my" as something less. It's like that old canned dog food commercial: "My my's bigger than your my. My my's better than yours." There you go: dog food psychology.

It's The Law

It gets complicated here. I'm going to talk mostly about people: individuals. The same rules apply to corporations and other organizations, but the whole concept of who's affected gets a lot more complicated than I want to get into. There's a point where a corporation is so big and influential that it can't help but affect everyone with anything it does, so there's no way for it to get consent to take any action at all. I don't think any corporation should ever get that big. Governments are naturally in that situation, and that's why we have to have elections. More on that in the last chapter.

If you think the above makes me all pro-government and anti-business, you haven't been paying attention. They're both hazards; it's just that at least government has a feedback mechanism built in. When businesses reach a certain level of power they overpower the elected governments that are supposed to regulate them, and the balance of power can tip the other way. I fear both an oversized government and an undersized government. I don't fear an undersized business.

Remember when I said that everyone has the right to do right, and no one has the right to do wrong? It gets hard to tell sometimes, what was right and what was wrong. It gets harder when you try to say, in advance, "this is always right" or "this is always wrong." Sometimes it comes down to the details of exactly how something happens. Yet getting it right, every time, *in advance*, is what we ask of the law all the time. It's why we need courts.

THE EMPIRE HAS NO CLOTHES!

Where I live there's a law against killing other people. Actually there are several, but there is another law which supersedes them all. If the defendant or suspect is found to have killed in self-defense, then they are not guilty because there was no crime. Unlike other "not guilty" findings, in matters of self-defense the case is closed. The murderer did not escape justice, *because there was no murder.* In lots of places, that same law protects me if I try to save *you* from a murder.

Now that's a pretty easy case. It gets harder and harder as the conflicts become more subtle. Could you imagine every possible circumstance where a usual wrong used to end a worse situation might be right? I certainly can't. No one can. Because humans are imperfect, we have to realize that the Law can never be perfect. The Law will either make criminal some things that may be right, or it will allow some things that may be wrong. In Statistics, these problems are called "false positives" and "false negatives," respectively. The goal is to keep both kinds of error as small as possible, but in something as broad and all-encompassing as law, there *will* be errors of both kinds because we just can't predict every possible situation. The question is, what kind of errors do we want to have?

We've decided that no one has the right to do wrong and that everyone has the right to do right. Also, no one has the right to forbid anyone the right to do right.

"Great! I can harass you with my religious/political/social beliefs all day and all night because they're right so I'm right!"

No, you can't. Harassing someone, causing them distress and taking away their time – part of their life! – is seriously impacting them. You don't get to push your ways on other people, and so long as they're not pushing theirs on you, just let it go.[43]

I believe that, for the most part, criminal law at least should err on the side of false negatives. "It's better that ten guilty people go free than

---

43 Practicing my own life and beliefs where you can see is not pushing them on you. Actively trying to make you participate, or repeatedly trying to force your attention, is. Let others be.

one innocent person be wrongly convicted." If we can't get it right, we should allow people to do right even if some unintentional wrongs are also permitted.

"Awesome! Stealing should be legal! I'm game!"

No, we're talking about far more subtle and difficult cases here. Cases of free speech, press, and pursuit of spiritual enlightenment and knowledge. Cases where the rights of individuals conflict. Cases where no parties are doing wrong until they are brought together and their actions interact with those of others.

So we have a guideline for writing the law: we should err on the side of allowing some wrongs in order to protect the right of all people to do right. It should err on the side of false negatives, allowing people the right to do right at all times, to make mistakes, and to not be tried as criminals for failing. At the same time, assaulting or harassing people for the way they live their lives is still assault or harassment.

Many places see the benefits of this and have what are known as "Good Samaritan" laws. If a person has current training in CPR, for example, and uses that training to try to save the life of another person, they cannot be tried in civil or criminal court if the recipient of their efforts doesn't revive.

Informed consent goes a long way toward changing a dangerous misadventure into a risky but well-managed pursuit. Licenses and permits are good for this kind of activity. Get a license to prove you know the risks and how to manage them, or sign a form that says that you have exercised due diligence in seeking out and understanding the risks you're taking, and you've taken responsibility for your actions. That form should cover all the types of risks so far discovered, to you and to others. No one gets to sue anybody if you get hurt or killed because it's your own fault. You took the risks for reasons and benefits you understood. And if you hurt someone who didn't sign on, it's your responsibility alone.

Keeping and bearing arms is one thing; bearing them in crowded public places is another; and having weapons of mass destruction are still another. No one would consent to having a neighbor, no matter how well respected, in sole control of a nuclear, biological, or chemical weapon. And what a find that would make for a burglar! The risk exposure there is amazing – and uncontrollable. Only governments that have the resources for the kind of controls we have to have to protect ourselves from us having them, should be allowed to have them, and I'm all for having a lot less of them.

The law should allow all forms of speech, press, and spiritual practice not proven or intended to do harm to non-participants. You want to hang yourself from a cross or self-flagelate? Painful and injurious, but if you find that the benefits to you outweigh the risks and costs, you should be allowed. Everyone else should have the right to ignore you. Want to commune with nature dressed only in what nature gave you? The same rules should apply, even in a municipal park. Want to assault or bully people? You're evil; you're doing and intending harm to others for no other purpose than to harm them, and the law has the right and the duty to stop you.

Put another way, the law has no place regulating what good people do among themselves for purposes that all affected agree are good. If certain people are offended by it, then they should ignore it. Just because something might be emotionally harmful for you, be it partner-swapping or eating tomatoes, doesn't mean it's harmful to those who practice it. It might, in fact, be a very positive-sum game for them. As long as they aren't forcing anyone else to participate or exposing non-participants to risks, and that's all clear to everyone around, you should move along and forget about it.

The Voice of the People

The most amazing thing about the voice of the people is that there isn't one. If you haven't noticed by now, we don't agree on everything. We can't even all agree on anything. So there is no "voice of the people." That's why we have legislatures: so they can disagree for us. Saves us the trouble of getting all upset at each other. Instead we just get upset at them. It must be a fun job! I can sure see how having everyone getting upset at me would make me happy.

Yeah, not so much.

There are voices among the conservatives that range from "we need to free and even subsidize business but heavily restrict individuals' private lives" to "all government is bad and must be eliminated." Voices among the liberals range from regulated business and free individuals to nationalization of certain industries. Both sides have their good ideas and their awful ones. With so much variation within parties, how can we expect that all of us of whatever party could possibly speak with one voice on anything? I think that if it were to happen, it could be a great thing or a terrible one, but we do need to try to understand each other and I don't see much of that coming from either side.

Social media give voices to all manner of people. Positions that don't align with any part of any party platform *per se* get heard. The cacophony is deafening at times, but we are hearing a lot more ideas and that's a good thing overall. Thankfully, a lot more is said than done.

THE EMPIRE HAS NO CLOTHES!

Online petitions allow people to band together on individual points where they agree. Probably no one petition tells us much unless it's **very** successful, but the lot of them together probably do. I'd love to see some good analysis on that.

With all that going on, it's no wonder that people don't seem to march as much as they used to. When they do, it's bigger news than it was.

American Elections are Un-American!

In an election between two Jedi and a Sith, the Sith will almost always win. The Sith gets 40% of the vote and the Jedi split the vote, 30-30. 60% of people want Jedi, but the Sith wins. Even if a quarter of one candidate's supporters vote "strategically" and switch to the other, it's still 37-23 against 40. The party with the least support still wins because it only fielded one candidate.

Now think about the way we do primaries, because they're way worse. In fact, if someone wins a presidential primary it's a fair bet that most of the time the winner isn't actually very popular. The more candidates there are in the race, the more likely it is that the winner is almost nobody's first or even second choice.

If there are 15 candidates, then all you need is about 6.5% support to be in the top half. Think about that: the front runner isn't likely to have much more than ten or twelve percent first-choice support! So then one of the candidates polling at three percent drops out. Maybe a quarter of their supporters have a second choice, and three quarters don't. The one quarter spread across the field, diluting themselves to near nothing across 14 other candidates. The others, knowing only that they don't want the Sith (the "other party") to win, for the most part fall in behind the front runner on the assumption that their party members are smart. They follow their Empire.

Because crowds instinctively follow the biggest, strongest, loudest

THE EMPIRE HAS NO CLOTHES!

male,[44] the front runner is most likely not the best choice – and almost no one's first choice. Now the 10% front-runner gets those lost 2-1/2% from the other candidate – and a 25% boost in his numbers. Even though only one in eight support this front-runner, that 25% boost *looks like a movement*. It isn't, but the way we do elections makes it into one.

Can't we do something about that?

Well as a matter of fact we can. There are two things we can do, and one of them follows the other.

Let's go back to our 15-horse race. If every state held its primary on the same day, that accumulation by attrition wouldn't happen. What *would* happen is that a lot of people wouldn't vote their conscience. They'd try to decide who their neighbors thought their neighbors thought most people would vote for. This is called *strategic voting* and it happens when people don't think their first choice has enough support to win and they really want to keep one particular candidate (or more!) from winning. They fall into that same old peer pressure. They become victims of the Empire, and we never know who would really win. Besides, someone could win with 7% support! It's even worse than the problem we set out to fix!

Einstein defined insanity as doing the same thing over and over and expecting different results. We've been voting the same way for 240 years and it hasn't gotten better. What if there were a way you could vote your true conscience without being afraid of spoiler effects? What if, if your candidate didn't win in that one day, you could drop the least popular candidate and have a runoff among the rest, and repeat that until someone had *an actual majority* of the votes? A bit arduous, but the results would be awesome! The primary would always produce a candidate with a genuine majority of support, not just the most support out of the five or six who remain.

---

44 There's lots of good research on this. It's actually pretty hard for people as a group to think past this instinct. A person is smart, but a bunch of people are still pretty stupid.

American Elections are Un-American!

We can make it even better. We can get all this done at once, and tell the winner exactly where their support came from, if we do all the runoff elections at once. It's called *Instant Runoff Voting*, and countries that use it see big increases in voter turnout and satisfaction with the system. On top of that, the influence of every voter, including a party's "core," which is actually a very vocal and extreme minority, becomes proportional to its numbers again.

But how do you have an instant runoff if you don't know who's lost? It's easy. When you go into the voting booth you "rank the candidates from first to worst." Stop whenever you run out of palatable candidates. That's it!

Counting is pretty simple, too, and computers make it workable. Before computers there was no way we could do it. It works like this:

1. Count all the first-choice votes.

2. Is there a true majority winner? If so, stop and announce!

3. Take all the ballots with the loser as the top choice and shift all the other votes up one spot. Continue at #1.

That's all there is to it. A straightforward analysis of the ballots can tell the winner where their second (and third and so on...) choice support came from. The will of the people is revealed in ways plurality elections just can't do! Mary, who came in second in the first and second rounds but got the majority in the third round, can find out that she got a lot of support from people whose first choice was Dave, and that she and Dave both got a lot of support from people whose first choice was George. That tells them – and the electorate – how all this really works, and because it's still a secret ballot, no one knows which person voted which way. All they know is that people who like George also like Dave and Mary, and that's a lot more than we know today.

We get better winners, and over time better candidates to choose from. There are other ranked electoral systems, but I really like Instant Runoff. It takes some special programming to keep the first, second, third, etc. choices together that some current American voting systems don't yet do. But IRV is the most familiar to the way we vote now, so it's easier for many to understand and accept and a great place to start the conversation.[45]

We can do this in the primaries without any changes to the Constitution. Each party can do it at any level since they control their own elections. Actually, since the states decide how they're going to do their general elections, we can do it at every level without mucking with the Constitution. We can even elect the president this way, though making it work with the Electoral College will take some thinking. I have a few thoughts on that but I'll save them for later. The point is that the poster child for electoral failure is the primaries, and we can make that change today.

If you want to "take back America" from special interests, then the way to do it is with our elections. Let's start electing local and state officials this way. Then maybe we can get the attention of the major parties at a national level and really fix our presidential primaries.

The first major party to go this way will have a huge advantage in that election, just for having better and more popular candidates on the ballots, as well as the electoral moral high ground. Let's get it done!

---

45 Since I finished writing this book I found out that Maine has voted to use Instant Runoff in its elections from now on! Maine is leading the way for improving American elections!

Beginnings and Endings

To get to the end I have to take you to the beginning. When I was two years old or so, I was quite a jerk. A "terrible two," to be certain. I laid it on to get whatever I wanted and often hurt people in the process. One day I still remember, in her anger and frustration my mother said, "think about how other people feel for a change." That was quite a revelation. You see, up until that moment I had thought that I was the only living, thinking, feeling thing there was; that everything else was just stuff. Here was my mother telling me that *other people have feelings*. It was a revelation and a revolution. In that moment I realized that all these people around me *were people like me*, that they had feelings *like mine*, and that meant a lot of things.

- People aren't just things in the universe like cars and trees and rocks and plumbing. They are living beings that work the same way I do.
- Most of them are older than I was, *a lot older*, so they've experienced more than I have.
  - They have feelings, and have felt more than I have.
  - They think, and have thought more than I have.
- People are all pretty much alike in a lot of ways because they're all made basically the same way.
- If all these things are true then I'm no more important than any other individual.
- There are a LOT of them, and only one of me.

151

THE EMPIRE HAS NO CLOTHES!

- ◆ The needs of the many outweigh the needs of the few. Or the one.

I didn't think any of that in words. It came in a flash, a visual explosion that rebuilt my model of my then still tiny universe. I wasn't alone, and I wasn't what the entire universe was all about. There are others like me. In that one moment my ethics were cast. I've been looking for the words for them ever since.

I believe that some people never need that epiphany. Some who do, never have it: they use the same words the rest of us do, and they talk about "other people," but the phrase never takes on the meaning it does for most of us. They never understand that other people are fundamentally the same as them. "Other people" is just a euphemism, if you will, for a certain class of objects in the world.[46]

I've had quite a number of epiphanies, or Moments of Revelation, mostly in my 20s. When I do, the processing power needed to rebuild *everything* so quickly leaves me blind and deaf for a few moments. In the days and weeks following each one I'm sure my friends just thought, "oh, he's changed his mind again." How right they were. I had changed my mind. Every bit of it.

Eventually that settled down and successive epiphanies rebuilt less and less of the model until everything fit together nicely. One big, coherent map of my universe.

There are still some things I can't do. I can't think of other people as property.[47] Trout don't own trout, foxes don't own foxes, and no member of any species has the right to own any member of the same species. I can think about people *thinking* of other people as property, though, and that gives me enough of a handle to work on the problem from a purely third-person perspective.

This book is the result of about a kryzlillion conversations with a

---

46 I can think of a few people who don't seem to have figured this out yet.
47 By that reasoning alone, corporations can't be people or have human rights because they can and do own each other. It's part of their function.

whole bunch of people over just about all my years so far. Many epiphanies. Many experiences. Many, many changes. I'm not the person I was at two, or eighteen, or thirty, or ten seconds before our$_F$ daughter was born. I'll continue changing, and learning, and finding new ways to explain things. I know I've forgotten a few things that should be in here, and my$_F$ wife has told me where I'd gone all Jack Kevorkian on you: taking 20 years to get somewhere and expecting everyone else to get it right off.

So many times in my life I've been amazed at how people just "didn't get it." The problem that immediately followed was that I couldn't explain it, either, so what could I expect? In 2002, my daughter looked up at me and for the first time asked, "why." I found my voice, wrote over 200 pages in six weeks, and didn't find a publisher. "Ethics in Our Universe" was never likely to be a bestseller. Boring title, and a drier writing style, but it does tell a lot more of how I arrived at my code.[48]

My purpose in writing "The Empire Has No Clothes" isn't to try to make you agree with everything I've said or what I think about this or that Emperor's clothes. My purpose has been to help you see the Empire, and its Clothes, for what they are: stories we tell ourselves to reaffirm our world view. We all see those clothes a little differently. When we realize that, we're able to consider whether we're telling ourselves the *right* stories, or whether we need to lay our Empire naked and see the real reasons. All of them. Maybe then the many spectra of our society and politics can see that like John Muir and Gifford Pinchot, we can *both be right* in certain circumstances and *both be wrong* if we try to apply those same standards universally. Left and right; authoritarian and libertarian; radical and preservationist; so many different spectra and we all fall somewhere on each of them.

Time was in America when if a member of one party was being a ass, members of both parties would work together to prank that person and make them lighten up a bit. Lately being a ass has been seen as a virtue. Like we used to do, let's reach out across the gulf that divides us,

---

48 I'm releasing it shortly after this book under the title "Equilibrium: Finding Our Way Through Right and Wrong"

THE EMPIRE HAS NO CLOTHES!

understand each other, find agreement, and when we can't let's disagree without being disagreeable. We don't have to call each other names just because we disagree. That's why I wear a Minbari Ranger pin: two sides of ourselves reaching across the gulf between us to join for a common cause.

About the Author

Grieg has lived in many places around the United States including Michigan, California, Illinois, Tennessee, Texas, Florida, Pennsylvania, and Washington, and traveled a little overseas. He's worked office, light industrial, construction, repair, management, and tech jobs. In the Marine Corps he graduated from Basic Training, Infantry Training School, and later, Officer Candidates' School. Along the way he learned a lot about himself and people in general. He's been an atheist, agnostic, pagan and born-again Christian, though not necessarily in that order. He calls himself fortunate to have had a direct part in saving four lives. He resigned in protest from the best job he ever had. It's been an exciting, if not lucrative life, but it's been lived with honor, integrity, and no small measure of fun.

He's moved 13 times in years starting with "2" and says he has "more right to hate moving than anyone but refugees." He's lost more money on his "last" homes than he'd care to remember. His genuinely last move he hopes will be to a boat where he can stop wasting his life making a living and start doing things that really matter.

He lives in the Pacific Northwest with his wife and daughter, and their black cat and overly friendly and excitable golden-shepherd-lab.

This and his first book, "Equilibrium," can be found on his website: www.griegpedersen.com/books

www.ingramcontent.com/pod-product-compliance
Lightning Source LLC
Chambersburg PA
CBHW050128280326
41933CB00010B/1289